AF525859

LINO GARCÍA MORALES

NEW MEDIA ART CONSERVATION

EVOLUTIVE CONSERVATION THEORY

Printing and Publishing: BoD – Books on Demand info@bod.com.es – www.bod.com.es Printed in Germany

ISBN: 978-8-4112-3522-8

OBSOLESCENCE NEVER MEANT THE END OF ANYTHING.

IT'S JUST THE BEGINNING.

MARSHALL MCLUHAM

AN OBJECT WHICH, IN AN ENVIRONMENT, EQUIPPED WITH FINALITIES, CARRIES OUT AN ACTIVITY AND SEES ITS INTERN STRUCTURE EVOLVING THROUGH TIME, WITHOUT LOSING ITS OWN IDENTITY.

JEAN-LOUIS LE MOIGNE

To Hugo, Héctor and Viki.

Contents

The End of the Restoration

If the restoration[1] is immanent to Art and "The End of Art" has been decreed, then there can be no doubt: Restoration has come to an end. As with Art, however, it is only a symbolic "End", the metaphor of a crisis.

Arthur Danto decreed the "End of Art", in the mid-1990s, proposing a story of art that collapsed at the moment when life and its representation became indiscernible. This in no way actually meant the absolute end of art, but rather a relative, theoretical, instrumental end of the hegemonic narrative.

There is no single, true, objective account of art. Rather, there is a set of more or less coherent, more or less accepted accounts that place works and artists into certain groupings, while excluding other works and artists that either do not fit in with the account or that theorists do not consider relevant or representative. Restoration, on the other hand, can have an alternative narrative based on the substance of the works of art, because Restoration is immanent to art and it is only this narrative that can avoid errors of logical classification.

[1] Restoration (capitalized) in this context refers to a set of activities common to conservation and restoration, in particular, and to many other activities related to exhibition, preservation, archiving, etc., in general. The main motivation is that they all share techniques, processes and strategies to maintain or recover the symbolic efficiency of the art object.

A story of art built on the substance of art[2] could be simplified to just three major overlapping periods of time, broken off from the others and coexisting today. For the purposes of the story told in this book, "traditional" art refers to what is otherwise called classical art, pre-modern art, the fine arts or, plainly, art, or even part of modern art, etc. It is the first stage of "art", whose origins date back to the Renaissance. In short, it is art produced according to a series of formal rules, in which there is a certain concern for the stability of matter and its permanence into the future; in other words, an interest in its conservation. This is what I mean by "tradition".

[2] Such a narrative would be valuable for Restoration though perhaps unimportant for the history of art.

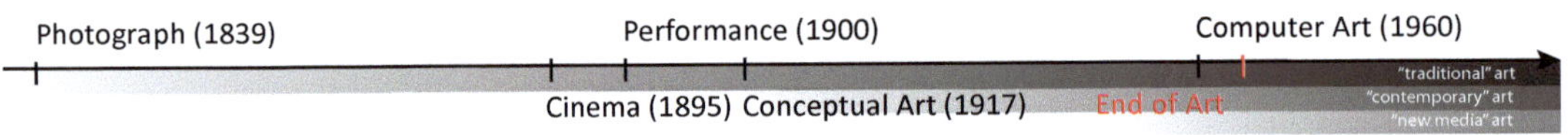

Figure 1: Fundamental milestones in the history of art.

This "tradition" was thrown into crisis by the desire to blur the boundaries between art and life. The emergence of photography in 1839, cinema in 1895, performance in 1900, conceptual art[3] in 1917, etc. (as shown in the Figure 1), gradually broadened the concept of what had hitherto been recognized as art. "Contemporary" art accepts that works can be reproduced technically and serialized (with the corresponding loss of the "aura"), it accepts ignoble materials and elements alien to tradition (any kind of element, without limits; elements that are more or less perishable, and more or less unstable), materiality disappears or shifts to a less important level, etc. In short, this art moves away from or relinquishes any previous standard "imposed" by tradition. Of course, the intention of many of these artists, and even of some movements, was to shatter the very concept of art (in whatever way they defined it).

[3] The definitive break with tradition, from a conservation perspective, came with the ready-made at the beginning of the 20th century. This term was coined by Marcel Duchamp to designate a reaction against retinal art (i.e., visual art) by an art that is learned through the mind, or conceptual art. As a current in art, however, "conceptual art" is associated with the later period of the 1960s.

What is referred to here as "contemporary" art[4], is certainly indebted to, and not entirely distinguishable from modern art; it is perhaps more appropriate to say that contemporary art ceased to be contemporary... since then.

The third period corresponds to "new media" art. Although the contemporary art object could already be active,[5] new media art introduces the digital computer, the metamedium par excellence, and completely expands reality. Similarly, instead of a clear and visible demarcation, I propose a diffuse period of electronic and technology-related art, of which it is heir. It could be said that this stage begins in the 1960s, at the height of contemporary art.

[4] Contemporary art is normally associated with the 1950s. Many of the terms used to name certain stages of art are defective and end up referring to a temporal period that is distanced from the semantic value of the term that names it.

[5] As is the case with film or performance.

The artwork as art object

To understand this story, it is necessary to define the substance of the artwork. From an ontological perspective, an artwork is an entity whose substance can be divided into two: *image* (which functions as an *aspect*) and *support* (which functions as a *structure*). This teleological divide may be irrelevant to the official story of art, but is fundamental to the Restoration.

The support is a *system*[6], while the image is a *symbol*[7]. The "symbol-object" is "text", the constituent discourse of the artefact, the content, meaning, or Gestalt, whereas the "system-object", the "testimony", what the text transmits, the container, the signifier, or Gestell. The work, as an object (system-symbol-object), is something abstract that is instantiated according to text/testimony, object-symbol/object-system, content/container. Fetishism, for example, confuses the object-system (part) with the object-system-symbol (whole).

[6] A *system* is a whole, formed by organized and interrelated parts. Everything outside the system is considered *context*.

[7] System of related signs whose function is symbolic.

This teleological division was proposed by Cesare Brandi in his Theory of Restauro. Matter, he says, is "that which serves the epiphany of the image" [Brandi, 2008, p. 13]. The support (system-object) is matter without which the image (symbol-object) is not possible. The support is restored[8] to the extent that it allows the epiphany of the image: by its end purpose, its telos.

[8] It could be said that the pupose of the Restoration, the end, is the *image*, not the *support*.

The proposed story of art, based on the technical nature of the artworks, is a discourse of dematerialization: from the passive material of fused support/image (which functions as structure/aspect), to the active material of dissolved support/image (where the structure is material and the aspect may be immaterial or hybrid); from the passive material of traditional art, which does not need energy to manifest itself, through a hybrid time interval (contemporary art) to the active material of the support (new media art) which needs electrical energy to manifest itself in an immaterial image. From this point of view it is a question of "things" that are not the same. Any of these members is not the same as its class, which is art. This is different from what happens in the other discourses. To consider everything as the same thing: as art, (i.e, to treat as more of the same, things that are not; to treat as class, object or as general that which is simply a member, subject or particular) due to the immanence of the Restoration with respect to its end, the artwork, is to commit an error of logical typification, which leads to a series of apparently irresolvable and incongruent paradoxes and confusions. But this is a story of art based on image; text, in Derrida's words. Image is figure, representation (from the greek *eikon*), likeness and appearance of something. It is imitation (from the latin *imago*), substitution, of some things for others. It is not reality, but the "creator" of unreality. It is not something, it is the absent represented in our mind. It is a sign. It can be material, deposited on a substrate, and it can be immaterial or hybrid (as in the case of cinema[9]).

[9] The image on the substrate is converted into light and is dematerialized to be contemplated. Likewise, sound is not matter, but energy.

Figure 2 illustrates this story based on the substance of the artwork. Traditional art is Image-Material. Both support and image are material. Everything is space. Contemporary art introduces movement and time. The Image: Movement or Time, can be material, hybrid or immaterial. New media art is fundamentally time: time-based art.

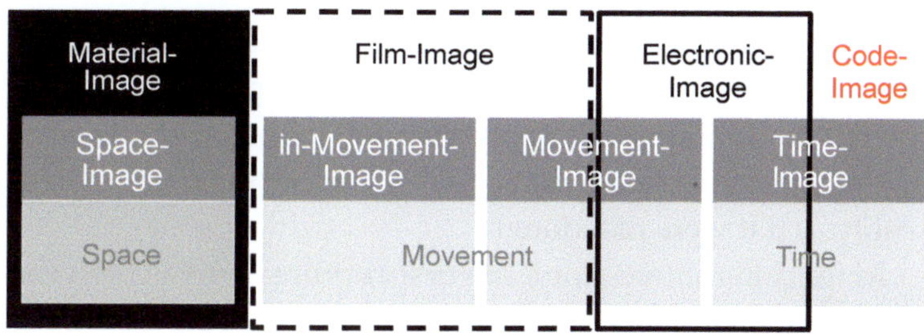

Figure 2: Image. The chronological sequence (read from left to right) shows the priority shift of the space to time, from materiality to immateriality, from the object to the process that leads to the object, from the fact to the event. It is a journey of superposition, conjunction, aggregation, and not exclusion, disjunction, substitution. In the Image-Material, materiality is everything, and the medium is the message. In the Image-Time, materiality loses relevance, the medium is diluted in the message. Materiality is only a support. The image is immaterial.

Figure 2 shows the relationship between the world of images of Henri Bergson [Deleuze, 1983, 1985] (Space-Image, in-Movement-Image, Movement-Image, Time-Image) and José Luis Brea [Brea, 2010] (Material-Image, Film-Image, Electronic-Image). The chronological sequence (from left to right) illustrates the priority shift from space to time, from materiality to immateriality, from the object to the process that leads to the object, from fact to event. The path is one of overlapping, conjunction, and aggregation, not exclusion, disjunction, and substitution.

In the information age, however, it is necessary to talk about Code-Image. Any "code" is a system of signs. Code-Image is virtual and the product of transcoding into the digital domain of any image corresponding to the Brea's "Ages" or of a computational generative process.

Code-Image is information, regardless of the support that contains it; it passes from one support to another, is multiplied through networks, copied, transferred, stored, processed, etc., without losing its essence or quality. In the Code-Image, all the copies are originals. The code is written in a formal language that was created by human beings, but to be processed by computers, not human beings.

Code-Image is the substance of new media. The computer interacts with the "real world" through its interfaces (commonly refered to as peripherals). It is the interface between the artist and reality, the instrument capable of altering the perception of reality as if it were playdough.

In this alternative story, the first rupture in art is between Image-Space and Image-in-Movement and the second important rupture is between Image-Movement and Image-Time (in Bergson's description). The image acquired its full autonomy and expanded its unreality in all its continuum (reality, augmented reality, augmented virtuality, virtuality); which encouraged processuality, interactivity, virtuality, ubiquity, etc.

Story of the Restoration

The "problem" of Restoration is a problem of the conservation/restoration of identity[10], of those properties or attributes and process of a work that make it different from all others and that define it as "unique". All theories try to define which are the limits that guarantee identity.

Restoration is a change that must ensure that the changed (restored) object remains the same, in that it retains its identity. Aristotle proposed a way to refer to anything in the world based on what he called "causes":

[10] The "state of authenticity" refers to the state in which actual identity is equal to real identity.

> 'Cause' means that from which, as immanent material, a thing comes into being [...], the form or pattern [...]. That from which the change or the resting from change first begins [...]. The end, i.e. that for the sake of which a thing is [...]. The same is true of all the means that intervene before the end [...], when something else has put the process in motion [...], for all these are for the sake of the end [...]. These, then, are practically all the senses in which causes are spoken of [...]. [Aristotle, Metaphysics, Book V, chapter 2].

The identity of the object,[11] therefore, is determined by its matter, form, efficiency and function. The material cause determines what a thing is made of; the formal cause, its disposition or form; the efficient cause, how it comes into existence; and the end cause, its function or purpose. According to Aristotle, if these four causes remain after the change, then the object remains the same.

[11] The object is system-symbol-object; however, if as Brandi proposes, the image is prioritized over the support (the latter only insofar as it satisfies the epiphany of the image), the identity of the object is determined by the symbol-object (image).

The Teoria del Restauro satisfies the demands of Traditional Art Restoration. Its pillars are authenticity, objectivity, universality and reversibility. In traditional art, support and image are inseparably bound: both are matter. The consideration of the conservation of matter and form, for example, is a priority, but only insofar as it shapes the image itself.

Muñoz Viñas's Contemporary Theory of Conservation places the subject, rather than the object, as the fundamental element of the Restoration. It is an anthropocentric theory, in which process (efficient cause) and telos[12] (end cause) are more important than matter (material cause) and the form (formal cause); and yet it can be applied to the Restoration of traditional art.

[12] If the restoration is done for the subject, the end cause, the symbolic value, is a priority.

The New Media Art Conservation Theory, or "Theory of Evolutive Conservation" proposed in these pages places "change" within the Restoration paradigm: *evolutivity*, permanence through change. The artwork can and must change, as long as it retains its identity.

This theory is shaped by a compendium of change-based theories that emerge primarily from the early initiative of the Variable Media Network [vmn].

This new media art conservation theory considers the particularities of new media art and can be applied to both contemporary and traditional art. However, in the case of objects whose support is material but whose image may be material, immaterial or hybrid, this theory places the obligation on the conservation of the identity of the image, not the support. The support is not the artwork itself, it is not the whole (system-symbol-object), but part of the whole (system-object). All of the causes are susceptible to change for the permanence of the image. The fundamental pillar of this theory is evolutivity, understood as that which allows the system-object to evolve.

Restoration is immanent, its end is the very object of Restoration, and it is united in an inseparable way to its essence. To avoid paradoxes and confusion, the logical levels or types must be strictly separated according to the substance of the image. Traditional art, contemporary art, new media art, etc., are members of the same class or group, which is "art"; but to consider new media art, for example, as a member of the traditional art class or the contemporary class of art, is to make an error in logical typification because traditional art, in this case, cannot be both member and class. In other words, although all the members of this story correspond to the art class, they are not all the same and cannot be treated as "more of the same". Each member of the class has its own substance which, as inherent to it, determines the Restoration. In other words, Restoring contemporary art or new media art as if it were traditional art is a mistake, and applying the Teoria del Restauro to a new media artwork is a mistake.

Reversibility and authenticity, two of the fundamental pillars of the Teoria del Restauro, do not make sense in the Restoration of contemporary art or the new media art.

To consider members Restoration of traditional art/Teoria del Restauro, or Restoration of contemporary art/Contemporary Theory of Restoration directly as the class "Restoration" is by the same token an error in logical typification.

Although there is a certain chronological hierarchy by which later Restoration "theories" can be to extrent absorb any previous theory, it cannot be said that they function as a closed system or universal class. Errors in logical typification set off unending game, lead to seemingly unsolvable and incongruous paradoxes, and throw the Art Restoration system in crisis. One could say that with these errors, we reach the End of the Restoration; as with the End of Art, however, its only marks a crisis, and it remains possible to envision Restoration after the End of the Restoration.

New Media Art Conservation Theory

Evolutive conservation is a paradigm of Restoration based on *permanence through change*. Circa 500 BCE, the Greek Philosopher Heraclitus of Ephesus, known as "the obscure ", warned that "there is nothing permanent except change." This trope has been repeated into the present, by philosophers such as Arthur Schopenhauer, for whom "change is the only thing that is immutable", and poets like Bob Dylan, in the aphorism, "nothing is as stable as change."And the metonymy, *permanence through change*, was inserted into the story of the Restoration by the Variable Media Initiative of the Guggenheim Museum in New York [Depocas et al., 2003].

All *change* is a transition that occurs when one passes from one *state* to another. The paradigm shift is resisted when it requires the shedding of habits that help maintain the balance or a certain situation. The basis of all change is the boldness to take the step to initiate it; but change is innate. Change is inevitable.

Contemporary art is as complex as it is unlimited. Any material or immaterial thing can be art; contemporaneity acts simply as an unlimited amplifier. New media art is an extension of that complexity expanded into unreality, progressive, ubiquitous, etc.

> [Artistic activity since the late 1960s] was governed by the principle, articulated by the two most influential artistic thinkers of that era, Andy Warhol and Joseph Beuys, that anything can be an artwork, that there is no special way that artworks have to look, that anyone can be an artist [Danto, 2010].

But not anything is Restorable. Some art objects are more conservable than others. It may be possible to define a certain "degree of conservability."

Evolutive conservation presupposes an "active" rather than a "passive" Restoration object. Jeff Koons's *Puppy* at the Guggenheim Museum in Bilbao (Figure 3) is probably the best examples of this type of conservation. *Puppy* was produced to mutate. Its characteristics are altogether uncommon: 13.8 meters in high, weighting 15 tons, with 38,000 flowers (including pansies in fall and winter, and begonias, impatiens, and petunias in spring and summer) grouped in small patches that are changed twice a year at a cost of €100,000 each time, the structure consists of layers of stainless steel sheets, an earthen substrate, geotextile mesh to fix the peat, access through an exterior door measuring 50 cms; a 5-tier internal scaffolding, homogeneous watering and fertilizing by means of a complex computer-controlled tube system that is activated daily, requiring a a team of 20 gardeners, 10 operators and a full-time specialist.

The flowers change continuously and are removed and replenished. The dog changes its image according to the fleeting conditions, but its symbolic efficiency remains unchanged. In spite of its continuous permutation nobody questions the *authenticity* of *Puppy*. Authenticity, the certification that testifies to the identity and truth of something, is not in thing's *structure* or even in its *aspect*. To better understand this concept, let's begin with a short introduction to the processes of Restoration for contemporary art.

Figure 3: Jeff Koons. *Puppy*, July 2010. Stainless steel, soil and flowering plants, (1240 × 830 × 910 cm). Guggenheim Bilbao Museum. Author of the photograph: Ardfern.

Restoration Theories

Theories of Restoration are not that old, and the practices of Restoration as they are known today began in the 19th century. All of the "traditional" theories ("classical" or "orthodox") that were systematized in preceptive texts (Brandi, Viollet-le-Duc, Ruskin, Boito, Baldini, etc.), make *matter* the *object of Restoration.*

"Contemporary" Restoration theories, on the other hand, are more dispersed, fragmented, expanding,[13] and consider the material, the immaterial and even the hybrid as their object.

[13] The Contemporary Theory of Restoration [Muñoz Viñas, 2003] is a valuable exercise in critical revision, ordering and systematization that is likely to become a "new" classic.

Restoration theories are the deontological rules of the profession. The are the discipline's "set of axioms", the set of rules that form the basis of knowledge and action. Yet even these evolve.

Conservation and *restoration* in cultural heritage are the set of processes used to saveguard and transmit cultural interest into the future. These processes "maintain" and "restore", respectively, the *efficiency* and *originality* of a product of human or natural activity, and their constittuent activities, such as examination, documentation, treatment, prevention and care, have been systematized, legislated and regulated for a subset of art that is pre-modern, and in accordance with certain canons (such as *authenticity*, *reversibility*, *objectivity*, *historicity*, etc.).

Conservation encompasses any activity that prepares a thing, through direct intervention, altering its non-perceptible characteristics (and perhaps some of its perceptible characteristics, in the existence of technical imperatives) to avoid or prevent greater alterations in the future. *Restoration* refers to any activity that aims to "return" the thing to its original or perceptible authentic state. Both processes are initiated only when necessary.

The Restoration of contemporary art must supersede but not negate the Restoration of traditional art and must resolve the crises and contradictions that this corpus imposes. Likewise, the Restoration of new media art must supersede but not negate the Restoration of contemporary art.

Exhibition is a "short-term" conservation process. Its fundamental objective is "to maintain" the efficiency of the thing for short cycles in close keeping with the restrictions and specific characteristics of the exhibition space. *Preservation* is a process that is routinely and incorrectly referred to as *preventive conservation*[14] and includes any indirect action on the environment that helps "maintain" the present state of the thing, and is therefore considered "long-term." *Documentation* is a residual activity that must be initiated from the moment of *production* as a support to all other processes and altered, and must be altered or updated by these processes. Whether *short-term* (production, exhibition) or *long-term* (preservation, conservation and restoration) all these processes, including documentation, can be included in the term Restoration, with a capital "R".[15]

Production and/or *documentation* affects the subsequent processes of *conservation*, *restoration* and *preservation*; and the weaker they are, the more they affect these subsequent processes. Seen from a different angle, not all the facets (within a broad range of productive permutability) of a system-symbol-object are equally *conservable*, *restorable* and/or *preservable*. The *progressive* nature of the "thing" requires it to mutate and adapt to the passage of time, and this must be incorporated into the productive process, from the beginning.

Evolutive conservation is nothing more than conservation that is predisposed to change, starting from the moment of the original *production* process or begun in a process of *recreation*. Restoration is only necessary, in this scenario, in the event of a breakage or general failure of system-object, but it is conditioned by the production process.

[14] "All conservation is preventive" [Muñoz Viñas, 2003].

[15] In [Muñoz Viñas, 2003], term Restoration is used to bind together all conservation/restoration processes; however, given the interrelationship and overlapping in all these activities, other terms should be considered.

Recreation is a Restoration strategy. See the Section *Restoration Strategies*, page 88.

"Recreation" is therefore a strategy that re-*produces*, and at the same time *documents* the thing. It generates a version, capable that can be conserved in an evolutive, permanence-through-change manner. The forementioned "predisposition" requieres the acceptance of a *long-term* "conservable" production option, which, in new media artworks based on the combination of the technological ingredients of the third industrial revolution (computing, communication, content), means a high resistance to technological obsolescence, i.e., a high capacity for adaptation to new scientific-technical developments. This is precisely what `A3` provides: a methodology to choose the "what" and the "how" rather the "which" of the system-object, its constitutive elements and their interrelationship within a paradigm that is well-suited to evolutive conservation: the paradigm of *complexity*.

Production as a Restoration Process

[16] Production at the intersection of art, science and technology has a complex and diffuse mapping. In this context, this extends to technological art, electronic art, multimedia, new media, etc.

The production of artworks using technology[16] is extremely complex in that it sits at the intersection of apparently irreconcilable areas of knowledge. Sculptural, print and pictorial techniques have been and continued to be expanded through the inexhaustible source of "new" tools and instruments provided by technological development. Photography, audiovisuals media (film, video, sound), computing, interfaces, the Internet, etc., have been progressively but inevitably incorporated into the process of artistic production.

[17] Whereas the components can be analog and/or digital, the *production* approach must be digital.

An artist whose works require electronic, analog, or digital elements of computing[17] has little recourse other than self-education and/or the externalization of some of the functions, and this cab lead to technical deficiencies or certain methodological weaknesses.

According to Laura Barreca, it is possible to approach the production of new media art thorugh a combination of the three main ingredients of the technological revolution of the 20th century: *computing*, *communication* and *content* [Barreca, 2008].

Computing includes any digital technology that consumes, processes and produces information; the computational element par excellence is the "computer", but it is not the only such element.[18] In this processual nature, the *medium* of computing also provides *interactivity* and *reactivity*. The maximum expression is *immersion*, which is a sensory extension that drives the mixing of real and virtual worlds. *Computing* carries important consequences in Restoration, which include *immateriality*, *reactivity* and *progressiveness*.

[18] The attribution of "intelligence" to certain devices, in a clear tendency towards massification (as for *ubiquitous computing*) is nothing more than a reference to this capacity for information processing.

Communication encompasses all technologies that allow the transport of *information* between two extremes (*nodes*); whether between processors, places, or people. The Internet, the network of networks, is the greates example: it is a technology that connects any two nodes on the planet and allows the transactions of information between them.

Content is closely related to *information* and its ability to reproduce certain aesthetic reactions. Information has undergone a great revolution, due in part to the processing capacity of computing and the information-movement capacity of by communication.

In the Internet of Things (IoT) paradigm, any device, no matter how small, has the capacity to process and transfer information. These "things" are the technological building blocks of present-day art production and recreation.

> [...] previously, creation came out of a scarcity of information and excess of knowledge; now it comes out of an excess of information and shortage of knowledge [Fernández Mallo, 2009].

Our world is now inmerse in the so-called third nature, or internaut life, where a gulf separates "the metaphysics of the brush and the pixel." *Computing*, *Communication* and *Content* are meta-ingredients of contemporary art and innovation is produced at their intersections.

First nature refers to agrarian life (pre-modern culture) and second nature to civic live (modern culture and first generation post-modern culture).

Artistic practices germinate like protozoan forms of life composed of metabolic and vital elements in full expansion-contraction, absorption-repulsion, definition-indetermination, emergence-death.

Poetics moves from utopia to heterotopia, from centers to the peripheries to the and fringes, from tradition to simulation –where wealth, permutation, dialogue abound– to a sphere of uncatalogued relations. The naming of these practices,[19] such as digital imaging, cinema, video, digital animation, interactive, digital installation, digital sculpture, virtual reality, augmented reality, robotic, net, software, computer, game, locative, artificial intelligence, artificial life (A-life), telepresence, digital music & sound, cell phone, etc., is associated with to the medium that is related to technology, which moves in space-time.

[19] In English it is only necessary to concatenate the word *art* after each element of the list and in Spanish just the opposite; with some exceptions such as *videoarte*.

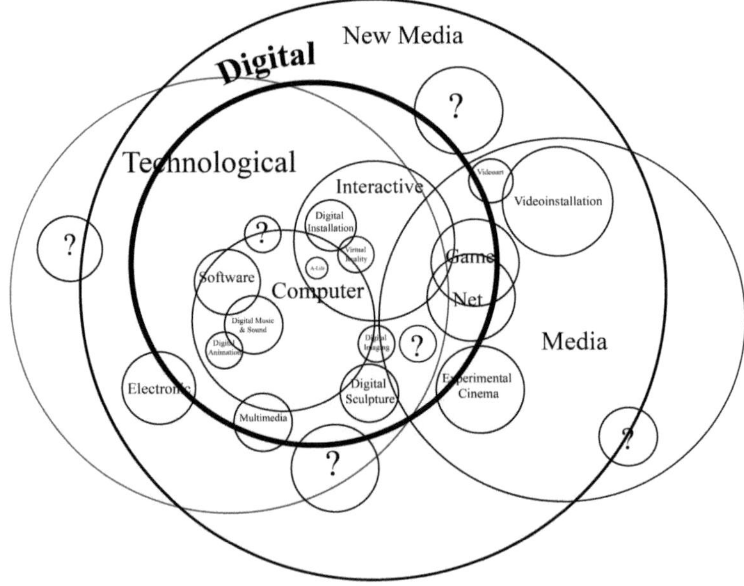

Figure 4: A cartography of new media art. This scheme is a compilation, based on the bibliography. In this book, digital art, software art and new media art are the same, but these classifications are elastic and vary according to who is doing the classifying.

Media that communicate with each other (*intermedia*), hybrid media that serve to create new media (*metamedia*), connect information (*hypermedia, hypertext*),[20] jump from one to another (*crossmedia*) or expand (*transmedia*) and offer the subject, not the spectator, not one story but many, with the capacity to explore alternatives, shortcuts and parallel paths and to influence their actions, similar to *ergodic interactivity* in events. Media that produce information according to the interaction with the receiving subject and, therefore, construct infinite multi-linear discourses and narratives (on a scale that is impossible for a single human being to explore).

[20] The *hyperlink* was created out of an overabundance of information. The result is a mechanism that allows you to quickly find and relate any data to any other data, without having to place in a linear or sequential fashion as the mind does.

> The greatest hypertext text is the Web itself, because it is more complex, unpredictable and dynamic than any novel that could have been written than a single human writer, even James Joyce [Manovich, 2006].

The interaction of Barreca "three Cs" acts as a meta-medium that generates new sets and sub-spaces with their respective osmotic boundaries and can serve as a guide in the identification of appropriate strategies in the production, preservation, conservation and restoration[21] of a given artwork. Seen from this perspective, production –as a process that generates the artwork– is not unique but multiple; in other words, it is possible to obtain the same system-symbol-object along with a broad capacity for permutability.

[21] all that which here is called Restoration (capitalized).

Authenticity, Identity and Truth

The starting hypothesis of conservation-restoration is to *maintain* or *recover* a certain *state of authenticity* $A = B$; where A is the objective state of authenticity of the object to restored (called *proto-state*) and B is the state of authenticity of the Restored object, in terms of efficiency or value.

However, the ambiguity in the interpretation of the concept of *authenticity* of an artwork alerts to the possibility of triggering a *historical falsehood*, and of turning a Restoration into a falsification of the work.[22]

[22] The main difference between *falsification* and *copy* is that a falsification pretends to be the *original*, while the copy seeks to be the original. A Restoration process does not produce a copy but an alteration of the "original". Falsification (fake) is understood as an alteration above and beyond an "authenticity threshold".

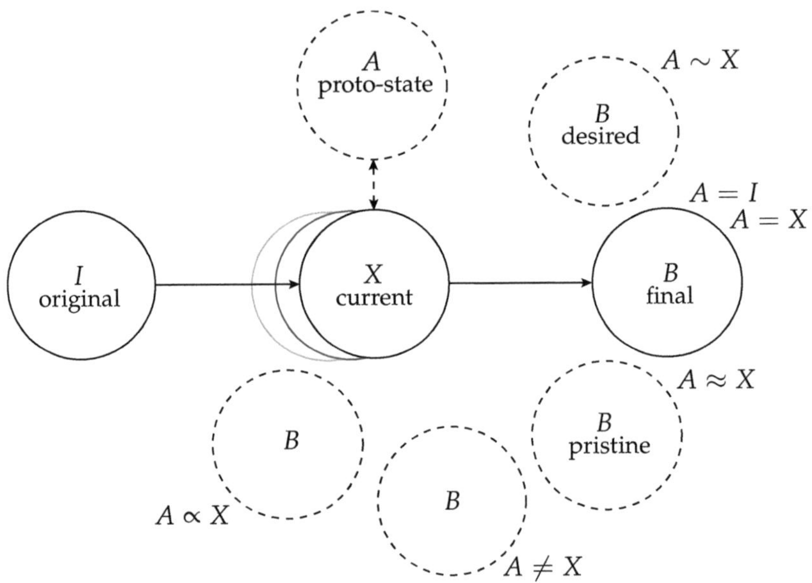

Figure 5: States of authenticity. I is the state of authenticity at the time of production, X is the state of authenticity at the time of Restoration, B is the final state, after Restoration; whereas A is the proto-state, target state of authenticity or reference state.

Authenticity is a certification that testifies to the *identity* and *truth* of something. It therefore depends on the concepts of *identity* and *truth*.[23] *Identity* is the set of traits that are proper to the object and characterize it in relation to others; that is to say, identity it is given by a series of properties that are unique to that object. From a scientific perspective, such properties are *intrinsic* to the object, measurable, objective, verifiable, whereas from the object-aesthetic point of view they are *extrinsic* to the object, immeasurable, subjective, unprovable. The basis of certainty is *evidence*. For Marina, "discovering the truth would be simple if each piece of evidence gave us information about its 'evidence strength', which is what provides us with a guarantee" [Marina, 1992, p. 232].

[23] "The meaning of the word *authenticity* is intimately linked to the idea of truth; that which is *true*, which is taken as truth, which offers no doubt, is authentic. Buildings and sites are material objects, bearers of a message or argument whose validity, within a given social and cultural context and its understanding and acceptance by the community, makes them patrimony" [A.A.V.V., 1995].

Truth, however, if it is to offer no doubt, to ceases to be *particular* and instead be elevated to the *universal*, must be *real*, understood as the fidelity of reality to itself, relieved of personal indications; unlike *particular* truth, which is based on private evidence. Truth as the "property that a thing has to remain always the same without any mutation" is a real, universal truth. For Muñoz Viñas, "appealing to *truth* or *authenticity* is a way of trying to turn decisions that are essentially subjective into objective, indisputable ones" [Muñoz Viñas, 2003]; evidence, however strong, lacks sufficient value. Any *symbolic value* refers to the aesthetic object, the image, the text, which are full of personal indicators; it is a question of particular or private truths.

The DNA of digital art, and of much of conceptual art, is *information*, which determines its identity and is imperishable. One could therefore say that the *authenticity* of a digital artwork is in the *information*.

There are four possible states of authenticity that can be reached [Muñoz Viñas, 2003]:

Original The state the object had at the time it was produced. Riegl proposes returning the its original state ($A = I$).

Desired As close to the current state as possible ($A \sim X$). Only by the authority of the artist is this a possible state. It does not correspond to any previous state and is a new state. In a sense, it is a reinterpretation of the object.

Current The state X the object has at the time of intervention. In Ruskin's view, for example, $A = X$ or $A \sim X$ (similarly equal). However, the historicity that burdens the *current* X state may encumber the selection of this state. This anti-restoration stance is know as non-intervention or minimal intervention. State of the object inmediately prior to its Restoration. In our time, the idea of maintaining the object at current state[24] still underlies much of Restoration theory.

[24] Ruskin's anti-restoration position: no intervention, minimal intervention, in which $A = X$ or $A \sim X$.

Pristine The state the object should have, though it in fact has never had (pure, ideal, perfect). It is a reinterpretation, warranted only by the authority of the Restorer and divorced from the authority of the author. It is Eugène Viollet-le-Duc's position: $A \approx X$ (approximately equal).

A is the proto-state or reference state.[25] The state of authenticity *B* should correspond to one of these four states above. At present, there are no scientific or objective arguments that determine what the optimum *final* state of authenticity must be, and therefore, the choice is purely *subjective* and should be agreed on by a multidisciplinary team, especially when invasive practices may be applied. However, in the Restoration of contemporary art and new media art, the state of authenticity to be determined is that of the symbol-object and not that of the system-object (a confusion commonly produced through an error of logical typification). My recommendation is to determine the proto-state that minimizes the deviation from the material, formal, efficient and end causes, with each one ascribed a weight in the study case.

[25] It is the state of authenticity chosen to be reached once the Restoration processes have been applied.

The *original*[26] is often unknown and therefore virtually impossible to determine. The state *desired* by the author, given single authority over the state of authenticity, is only possible in properly documented cases. The *current* state requires hardly any action. The *pristine* state is in reality a reinterpretation of artwork; by the Restorer or even by the author of the work.

[26] or *initial* state.

There are two basic types of difference:

Class It is based on the fundamental type under consideration (different types); it indicates different orders, groups or species of things and is marked by discontinuities or qualitative leaps.

Grade Variations between things that are intrinsically very similar, that indicate differences within the same order, group, species and imply continuity or quantitative leaps.

Equality, however, is not absolute. $A = B$ relative to something, be it material, form, efficiency, and/or end. If $A = B$ for all of the causes, one could say that there is really no difference between the two and, therefore, *identity* is produced. The *identity of indiscernibles* is the name given to a variety of philosophical principles proposed by Gottfried Leibniz sometimes also know as *Leibniz's law*. These principles are, principally:

- If two objects A and B share all the same *properties*, then A and B are identical; that is to say, they are the same object.
- If two objects A and B share all their *qualitative properties*,[27] then A and B are identical.
- If two objects A and B share all the same *non-relational qualitative properties*,[28] then A and B are identical.

Using the *identity principle*, we known that the object B has the property of being identical to itself, i.e. to B. If we then suppose that A and B share all their properties, then A will also have the property of being identical to B.

The earlist known definition of identity: "whatever is, and what is no cannot be", is attributed to Parmenides de Elea, a pre-Socratic philosopher of ancient Greece who lived between 530 and 515 BC. This sentence is interpreted as expressing what remains in spite of changes, as similarity to itself out of time, and that which remains identical. This thought arose in response to the metaphysics that another Greek philosopher, Heraclitus (535-484 B.C.), who concluded that a thing could be and not be at the same time; "no man steps in the same river twice" because "everything flows."

[27] Intuitively, a qualitative property is an intrinsic property to objects, which can be instantiated by more than one object and which does not involve a relationship with any other particular object. For example, color property is subjective, not qualitative, unlike the number of sides of a figure. Qualitative properties are intrinsic to objects and can be applied to more than one without involving a relationship to any other particular object.

[28] Not every qualitative property is non-relational, because some relational properties do not imply a relationship with a particular object. For example, the property of being on a table, any table.

In analyzing the idea that a thing could be and not be in a constant becoming, Parmenides understood that this logic presented a contradiction: "that the being is not; that the one who is, is not; since what is in this moment, is no longer in this moment, but becomes something else".[29] For Leibniz, the identity problem is articulated on Parmenides and Aristotle's *principle of non-contradiction*. He argues that it is innate, in other words that it is found in the human soul to be in the same sense, without needing to have been learned. "The contradiction principle includes two true enunciations: the first, that a proposition cannot be true and false at the same time; the second, that a proposition cannot be neither true nor false."

[29] Consequently, he elaborates a philosophy based on three principles: "the Being is the Being", "the Being is not the non-Being" (non-contradiction principle) and "the Being cannot be and not be at the same time" (principle of the excluded third). This thought about the condition of the Self became a philosophical premise still in use today.

> *Identity* has been approached from classical philosophical thought to the new currents of contemporary interdisciplinary sciences, setting up what is known today as a *complex notion*, an inexhaustible source of questioning in different fields. Part of its complexity is that it contains two opposite concepts: the fixed and the mutable. On the one hand, it is related to the belief in essences, with essential realities, substances that are both immutable and original; and on the other hand, that there are no eternal essences because everything is subject to change. At present, although both concepts coexist, the balance leans towards a definition of mutable identity, which is constantly changing due to its inherent relational quality: identity is created in experience with others [Chamorro, 2011].

The introduction of the *identity principle* is often attributed to Aristotle, but no reference to it exists until after Thomas Aquinas in the 13th century. In the 17th century, reference to this law was common among philosophers, and it is likely to have been taken from the teachings of Aristotle during the late Middle Ages. Friedrich Hegel subjected the *identity principle* to radical criticism. For Hegel there is a passage from the first A to the second, in the proposition $A = A$.

"Identity is not self-evident, it is affirmed." The second A is outside the first. *Identity* contains *difference*. The new logic proposed by Hegel is not, however, based on the *identity principle*, but on the *contradiction principle*. A contradiction is established that must not be rejected or denied, but fully assumed and reconciled.[30]

On the *identity principle*, Ludwig Wittgenstein commented that A implies non-A; he thus relates identity-diversity. That is, for every A there must also be something that is non-A. Wittgenstein uses this principle to defend his thesis that the set of rules that make up a grammar is absolutely arbitrary;[31] he asserts that "saying of two things that they are identical is meaningless and saying one thing that is identical to itself is not saying anything." Thus, he demolishes the previous thesis by saying that "we can first conceive of two objects as separate and then merge them with thought into one."

For Alfred Korzybski, the founder of *general semantics*, "no two Hardvard men, no two Ford cars, no two mothers-in-law, no two politicians, no two leaves from the same tree, are identical in all aspects." Yet it is clear that a student, not the Ford car, a mother-in-law and a leaf from the same tree are all identical to themself and maintains their genotype from birth to death; so that identity, as a *complex notion*, when subjected to change, is not fixed but mutates.

If B is approximately equal to A ($A \sim B$, $A \approx B$) (in all respects, and within a critical range or interval), in terms of *differences of degree*, rather than class, one could say that it maintains its *value*. This distance is proportional to the differences in degree between the properties of the original object A and Restored object B. If $A \neq B$, then B is false; that is, the Restoration process can be considered failed. This is precisely the justification for *reversibility*.

[30] If A is B, A depends on B, which in turn denies it, contradicts it. Therefore, thought A is realized when it is denied by B. In short, this proposition is equivalent to the affirmation that A is A, in struggle with B.

[31] This is known as justification on the basis of polarity argument, which determines that no declarative sentence can justify a rule of a grammar: if a sentence has meaning, its negation must also have meaning, and if a sentence justifies a rule, its negation should also do so, which is absurd.

If the processes applied are irreversible, it is not possible to return the object to its current state; however, in many contemporary art and new media art practices, it is very difficult if not impossible to apply completely reversible processes to the symbol-object.

All these ideas around $A = B$, when A and B are an *object* or *thing* that exists as material or objective, can be articulated on a series of properties that are unique to that object, such as shape, texture, color, tone, material, and on differences in degree; but how can these be implement when A and B are *concept*, i.e. immaterial or subjective? The concept of a thing does not include the diversity of the thing. Concepts are constructions or mental images. A *cognitive unit of meaning* is considered to be a mental content that is sometimes defined as a "unit of knowledge". According to Haroldo Gallo, "a thing can be said to be authentic when there is a correspondence between the *object* and its *meaning*" [Gallo, 2010].[32] The authenticity of the symbol-object, regardless of its material or immaterial nature, can be determined by its *symbolic value*, and *authenticity of meaning*. In short, it is possible, generically, to treat the object as a concept.

[32] According to Ferdinand de Saussure, *meaning* is the *mental content* that is given to a *sign*. In semiotics, the *sign* is a basic unit constituted by a *signifier* and a *signified*. For Charles S. Peirce, the *signified* is the interpretation of the sign or representamen; that is to say, it is the *concept* or *idea* that is associated to the *sign* in all type of communication, as it is the *mental content* and this depends on each person, since each one assigns a *mental value* to the *signified*, but by convention this *signified* must be equal for optimal communication.

One of the best examples to illustrate the problem of continuous identity is the Ship of Theseus paradox, from a Greek legend told by Plutarch:

> The ship wherein Theseus and the youth of Athens returned from Crete had thirty oars, and was preserved by the Athenians down even from the time of Demetrius Phalereus, for they took away the old planks as they decayed, putting in new and stronger timber in their places, insomuch that this ship became a standing example among the philosophers, for the logical question of *things that grow*; one side holding that the ship remained the same, and the other contending that it was not the same.

At that time in history the ship was still in Athens, but everyone agreed that it did not contain a single fragment of that ship in which Theseus returned from Crete.

It was repaired and recomposed so many times that, as Robert Graves explains, "philosophers cite it as an example when discussing the problem of *continuous identity*." The problem of *continuous identity* is, of course, the same as the problem of *changing identity* (liquid): what is it that makes a thing remain the same thing in spite of changes? For many Athenians, that ship was no longer Theseus's ship, because he did not keep a single piece of the original. For others, it was, because its form and finality were the same.

What would happen, as Daniel Tubau wonders [Tubau, 2012], if the replaced parts were stored, and then used to rebuild the ship. Which one, if either, would be Theseus's original ship? The Ship of Theseus paradox is a replacement paradox that questions if, when all of the *parts* of an object are replaced, it remains the same. It is as old as the opposite view of metaphysical identity that Heraclitus asserted: "No man can cross the same river twice, for neither the man nor water will be the same."

In eastern philosophy, however, the *identity problem* is understood from a different perspective. In Asia, the Ship of Theseus is probably not a paradox. In *Last Chance to See*,[33] Douglas Adams wites:

[33] Published in 1991 with Mark Carwardine.

> I remembered once, in Japan, having been to see the Gold Pavilion Temple in Kyoto and being mildly surprised at quite how well it had weathered the passage of time since it was first built in the fourteenth century. I was told it hadn't weathered well at all, and had in fact been burnt to the ground twice in this century. "So it isn't the original building?" I had asked my Japanese guide.
> -But yes, of course it is, -he insisted, rather surprised at my question.
> -But it's burnt down?
> -Yes.
> -Twice.
> -Many times.

> -And rebuilt.
> -Of course. It is an important and historic building.
> -With completely new materials.
> -But of course. It was burnt down.
> -So how can it be the same building?
> -It is always the same building.
> I had to admit to myself that this was in fact a perfectly rational point of view, it merely started from an unexpected premise. The idea of the building, the intention of it, its design, are all immutable and are the essence of the building. The intention of the original builders is what survives. The wood of which the design is constructed decays and is replaced when necessary. To be overly concerned with the original materials, which are merely sentimental souvenirs of the past, is to fail to see the living building itself.

Theseus's ship, in a limited sense, can be described as the same ship, due to the formal cause, or design, even though the material used to build it may vary over time. Likewise, a river has the same formal cause, even though the material cause (the water contained in it) changes over time. Theseus's ship could have the same purpose, i.e. to transport Theseus, even though its material cause may change over time. The efficient cause, how the craftsmen made and assembled the ship, could be the same: the workers who built the ship in the first place could have used the same tools and techniques to replace the ship's planks. The efficient cause (the craftsman) builds with the final cause in mind and has considered the formal cause, of course, using the material cause (for example, the same type of wood, even if it is not from the same tree).

Aristotelian causes say a lot about the identity of thing; but don't say everything. That *thing* can be an *object* or a *conceptual object*. In any event, the causes, which can be applied to the whole, to the system-symbol-object, are much more relevant when they are applied to the image, text, or surface of the object that produces the sensory experience.

In the example of the Gold Pavilion Temple in Kyoto, the objects are defined not so much by their form (formal cause), but by their function (end cause). The different *attributes* of the *causes* can form *classes;* however small variations of an attribute and differences in degree do not constitute a difference in class.

A common argument based on philosophical literature is that we are dealing with two definitions of the "sameness." On the one hand, things can be *qualitatively* the same, only for having the same properties. On the other hand, they could be numerically the same as "one."[34]

The main problem with this solution is that if we make our own definition of identity broad enough, *qualitative identity* collapses into *numerical identity*.[35] Since nothing can be qualitatively different, without also having to be numerically different, the thing has to be numerically different at different instants of time. According to Hayakawa:

> Most of our valuation errors arise [...] from *identification reactions*, in which we ignore the differences between individuals of the same class name, and in which we ignore the changes that occur over time.

Identification reactions can lead to an error in logical typification when the art object belongs to a class that is "art ... ", which is assumed as more of the same, ignoring not only the changes produced over time but the variation in the very substance of the individual being named.

[34] Think for example of two bowling balls that are "seen" as identical; they are qualitatively but not numerically the same. If one of the balls were painted a different color, it would be numerically the same as it was before, but not qualitatively the same as its partner. This is why there cannot be two Harvard students, or two Ford cars, or two mothers-in-law, or two politicians, or two leaves from the same tree that are identical.

[35] For example, if one of the qualities of the bowling ball is a space-time location, then there cannot be two balls in different places and times that can ever be qualitatively identical, since they have different properties at each instant of time (such as different speed). They can never be qualitatively identical at different instants of time.

Identification implies a certain expectation: something that fits our concepts. Some people will see things (materialistic), not concepts (idealistic). There is a tension, therefore, between quantity, objectivity, and quality, subjectivity, that is given by one's perception. What concerned Korzybski most was how language modifies perception. "One cannot perceive the world directly." The outside world is perceived thanks to the nervous system, but that worldarrives *translated, adapted*. According to Kant: "It is not possible to know the thing itself (the *noumenon*), only the *phenomenon*." In the outside world, for example, there are no colors, as we perceive them, only wave vibrations that can be translated into different perceptions depending on wether the person is colorblind or not. To Korzysbki, our sensations and perceptions are also contaminated by the structure of language.

Figure 6 shows Korzysbki's structural differential. The *parabola* represents the *noumenon*, i.e. the things that cannot be directly perceived. The *circle* is what is perceived, not the thing itself. It represents the reactions of the nervous system to that outside world. The *rectangle* represents the world of words that serve to identify the things perceived. The *holes* in each geometric figure represent the characteristics of each level and the *strings* between holes of different levels link those elements that have been abstracted from the upper level. The holes that have no strings are unperceived characteristics. The strings that come out of a hole and go nowhere represent the structure of *reality*.[36] The strings that go from the third level to the first represent *concepts, abstractions* that deduce how the world of level one could be even though none of its effects have been perceived in level two. The appellation Theseus's ship does not change but the ship does: it is destroyed if we forget about it.

[36] What should be perceived but has not yet been perceived or what are perceived but have not been assigned words.

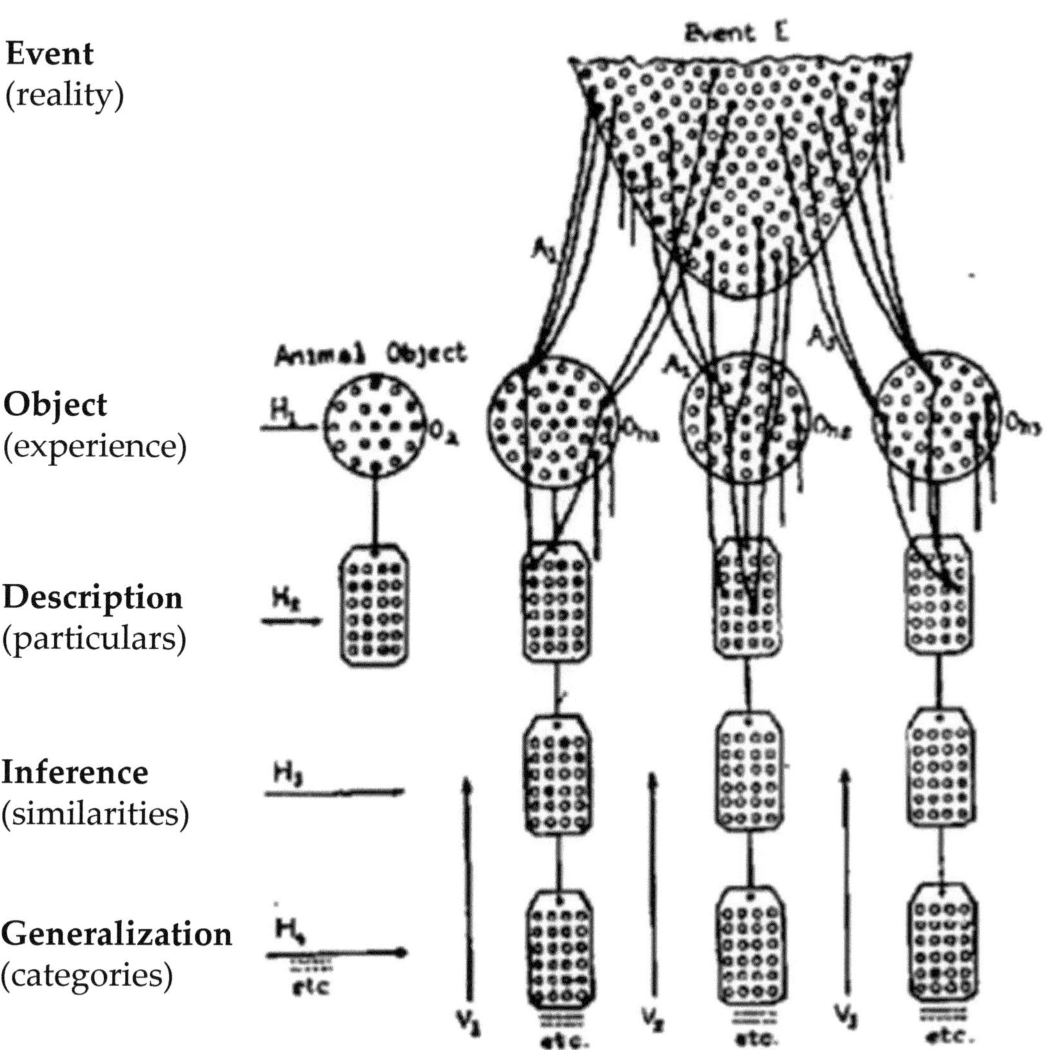

Figure 6: Korzybski's Structural Differential.

The influence of perception in the representation of reality is perhaps the most plausible justification that *differentiates* an artwork *A* from an "identical" object extracted from everyday life *B*.[37] Figure 7 is probably Warhol's best-known sculpture, a silk-screened replica on wood of the boxes of a popular detergent. *Brillo Boxes* were part of a series of sculptures representing objects that were typical of a neighborhood market, such as Heinz ketchup or Campbell's Soup Cans.

[37] Knowledge of the artist's intention (non-discernible difference) conditions the receiver's judgment. If the artist is a *brand*, if the gallery where it is exhibited is a *brand*, if the criticism is a *brand*, if the artworks of this artist are sold for large sums of money, if the work has belonged to important collections, doesn't the work begin to be considered differently? Wouldn't nonexistent aesthetic qualities be considered? Wouldn't an economic value be given to an artwork that it didn't have before? These attributes, however, are all extrinsic to the artwork, projected onto it.

Figure 7: Andy Warhol. *Brillo Box* (soap pads), 1968. Synthetic polymer paint and screen printing inks on wood, dimensions: 44.2 x 44.2 x 36.3 cm.

The argument over *equality* and *difference* has unleashed what Joseph Margolis calls a "closet scandal [...] in the philosophy of art." [Margolis, 2003] According to Nelson Goodman, the difference between a true work of art *A* and a forgery *B* is always through a difference in perception that (sensorially) "no one had ever noticed before" [Goodman, 2010] (sensorially). According to Margolis this statement is arbitrary and false. For Goodman, the decisive question of why there is any aesthetic difference between a good forgery and the original artwork is a challenge to the basic premise on which depends the very functions of the collector, the museum and the art historian depend; that is, *authenticity*.

According to Arthur Danto, what distinguishes an artwork as such is completely indiscernible by perceptual means. There may be no difference in perception, discernible through the senses, between an artwork and just a real thing, or between two totally different artworks [Danto, 2010]. There are always *indiscernible differences* between these examples, related to the history of their production and to the artist's intention. For Danto, artworks and objects cannot be identical because the former have been attributed intentional properties and the latter are not; "to see something as art requires something the eye cannot see [...] an atmosphere of theory." According to Margolis the assertion of non-discernible attributes, extrinsic to the work itself, is incoherent and paradoxical in extremis. False in the sense of "see" or obfuscated: discounting the role played by the theory of the perception of physical objects. The *"sensory" indiscernability* is found within the space of physical changes in the activated organ.

According to Margolis a work of art *A* and its fake *B*, cannot be characterized except in terms not restricted to any just material, sensory or semiotic properties. For Margolis the allographic depends on the autographic (notation, style, distinctive aesthetic properties):

"[...] reference, denotation, identification and reidentification, cannot be captured in principle by marely predicative means."[38] Just as Leibniz discovered: two things that are numerically distinct cannot possess the same general attributes.

[38] Predicate is that which is affirmed of the subject in a proposition.

> [...] the allographic use of scores is logically designed to serve whatever prior independent denotative and individuate competencies may be counted on –which, in context, can be other than autographic. [...] there is no known solution for the cognitive grasp of predicative similarity.

The focus of this dispute is "whether *undiscernible differences* count as, or contribute to, *aesthetic differences*." Indiscernible differences (intentional properties) are extrinsic to the object and, in Margolis' view, should not count as aesthetic differences.

For the recognition of authenticity the condition, therefore $A = B$ should be necessary and sufficient, but it is not; in "contemporary" art authenticity is generally based on both differences: discernible (perceptual) and non-discernible (intentional). In the Restoration, $A = B$ is a necessary and sufficient condition to reach a true authentic state; but this happens rather excepcionally, such as when "recreating" the lost image of a videoinstallation. In most cases $A \neq B$. Clearly, Restoration is not innocuous and even when it is reversible the Restorer leaves a kind of trace or distinguishable feature that prevents confusion.[39] In other words, reaching the state of authenticity $A = B$ is viewed as committing a falsification.

[39] For example, *tratteggio* or *rigatino* in chromatic reintegration; not visible at a distance, they uses color frames (primary colors, normally) that are distinguishable at a short range.

In all cases, the object of Restoration starts from an initial authentic state I, passes through an authentic state X and reaches the final authentic state B. The evaluation of "truth" depends on the *chosen* strategy to evaluate authenticity (more or less liquid).

Why $A \neq B$? So far, different approaches to *authenticity* have been analyzed. Why doesn't Leibniz's law enough? Danto points out that certain *indiscernible differences* or differences that are *extrinsic* to the object, such as the artist's intention or things related to the history of the production of the object, introduce *aesthetic differences*. Other authors, such as Margolis, do not. Be that as it may, this equation is incomplete.

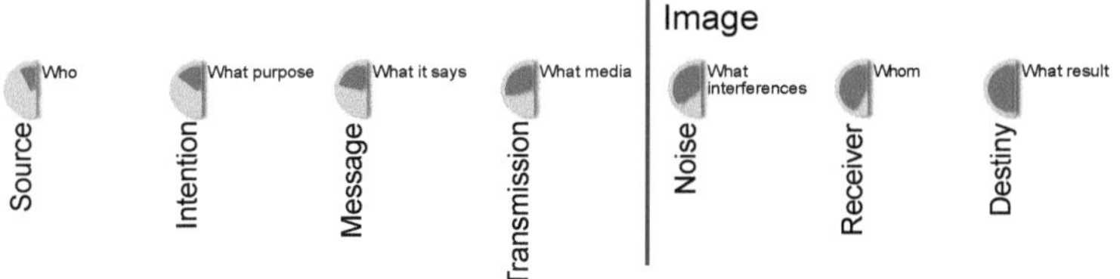

Figure 8: Reality and perception.
Using *Brillo Box* as an example, Andy Warhol is the *source* (*who*); whose *intention* is to show consumer objects as art (for *what purpose*); as *message* he chooses a commercial product (*what it says*); for its *transmission* he reproduces it in wood (with *what media*); the *noise* is given by its exhibition in a contemporary art gallery and by the halo that surrounds the artwork (*what interference*); the *receiver* is a collector who buys the artwork (to *whom*); and as a end point (*destiny*) the collector exhibits it in his house (with *what result*). All this, notwithstanding that what is exhibited is only an interpretation.

In the semiotic chain, the *image* is treated as a *sign* and includes a process of contemplation whose function is to decipher signs but the relationship between *signifier* and *signified* is arbitrary and

> the play of signifiers allows for all sorts of rhetorical juggling. [...] Multiple expansion is the fate of every system of symbolic exchange. Signifiers reproduce themselves more quickly than signified, causing inflation, *barroquismo* and formal sophistication [Marina, 1992].

The symbolic value of an object is cleverly reworked under the guise of *brands* play: "[the object becomes] an ontological hybrid that retains its physical characteristics, that are detached from its real references", in a "dream". The receiver is the missing variable in this complex equation: the conditioned receiver. The noise, as if it were a game, alters the essence of things: the king puts on the invisible garment and emerges naked.

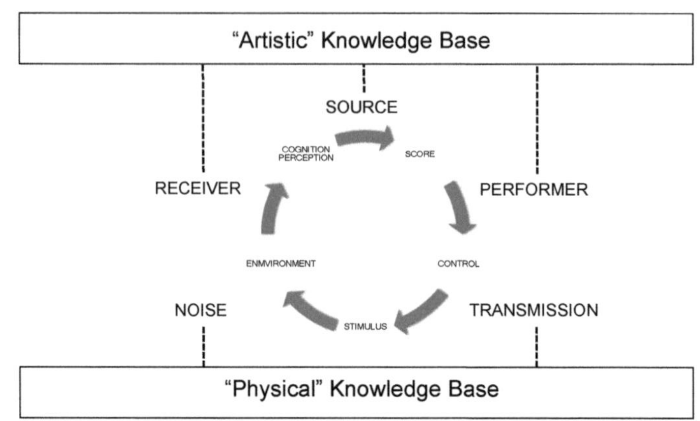

Figure 9: Adapted from the Richard Moore's Knowledge Base.
In the original model the system processors are: *composer* (*source*), generates musical data in some system of symbolic representation, using abstract musical information); *performer*, consuming abstract musical information and transforming it into a series of control actions on the instrument; *instrument* (*transmission*), receiving certain control actions which it transforms into sound); *room* (*noise*), producing a sound field from the sound according to its acoustic properties; and *listener* (*receiver*), capturing acoustic information from the sound field and processing it through his/her perceptual and cognitive system to produce abstract musical information. The higher-level processors –*composer*, *performer*, *listener*– constitute the "musical" knowledge base (*who*, to *whom*); while the lower-level processors –*instrument* and *room*– constitute the "physical" knowledge base (with *what media*, with *what interferences*).

Richard Moore proposed a model between source and receiver in terms of information, which sequences data and processes (transformers of that data) in a circular order [Moorer, 1990]. The "universalization" of this model, represented in the Figure 9, shows the artist (*source*) as a processor that intentionally generates a message in some notational system (*score*) from a set of mental representations. The *performer* consumes this information and transforms it into a series of *control* actions on the *transmission* medium to generate certain *stimulus*: the (sound, visual, tactile, etc.) image. The representation takes place in some space-time that generates *noise* (usually the "white box", although not necessarily) and interferes as a *field* (transfiguration of information) where the *receiver* is immersed, and the receiver captures it and transforms it into *sensory* and *perceptual* information at a lower level, and *cognitive* information, at a higher level. This information serves to close the cycle and provide the *source* with search patterns in doing new projects.

Note that this "universal" model gives rise to *allographic* practices such as music, dance, architecture, or theatre, and *autographic* practices such aspainting, sculpture, etc.

Both *source* and *performer* can be, but aren't no necessarily, the same person.[40] Allographic practices require a system of symbolic notation or, if rigorous authenticity is not a priority, at least a *plan*. The *proof of authenticity* in allographic arts lies in the accuracy of the transcription in a given notation. A notational system is much more than a simple plan or method and must satisfy five requirements [Goodman, 2010]: *non-ambiguity* and the four combinations that produce *disjunction* and *differentiation*, *syntactic* and *semantics*.

The adaptation of Moorer's model is closely related to the semiotic model of the Figure 8 (where *source*, *intention* and *message* are compressed into a single *source* or *source–perfeormer* and *destiny* appears linked to the processes that close the *receiver–source* loop) fittingly representing both processes and data as a single thing: *information*. Information is not perishable; and this principle is one of the pillars of the New Media Art Conservation. All this information belongs to cultural heritage and can therefore be an *object of Restoration*. When the symbolic value is well defined by the information one might even call it *informational conservation* [Muñoz Viñas, 2003].

Figure 10 shows a number of non-conventional music "notation" systems, reinvented to overcome what were seen as the gaps, deficiencies and inadequacies of the traditional notation system in the representation of the possibilities of sound new technologies offer. The loss of the function, however, in the failure to satisfy Goodman's requirements (non-satisfaction of non-ambiguity, disjunction and differentiation, syntactic and semantic) relegates them to simple visual poetry. Figure 11 shows a practical example of the dance notation system proposed by Laban [Newlove and Dalby, 2008].

[40] A plan for the production of Sol LeWitt's drawing #541, for example, requires a performer. The notation acts as a certificate of authentication. "It is well known that Damien Hirst [the world's richest contemporary artist] does not make his works: a group of collaborators is commissioned to do so. They are the ones who made, for example, the 25,781 one-millimetre dots without repeating a single color that make up one of his pieces. For Hirst, it is the idea that is important, not its physical materialization. That's why he considers it normal that, as has already happened, if one of his famous sharks suspended in a formaldehyde container rots, another shark is placed and that's it. The fact that this artwork can be considered a copy, and not an original, is incidental. Its value remains intact. But, in that case, why pay 12 million for a shark when you can buy it for much less? And who can assure us that the artist has not copied that same idea" [Oppenheimer, 2012]. And so it is for an artist, for example, who in general does not need a notational system for his project and acts directly on the media. Yet in the art tradition, both processes are well differentiated from their own genesis and in contemporary art it is, not surprisingly, a usual practice.

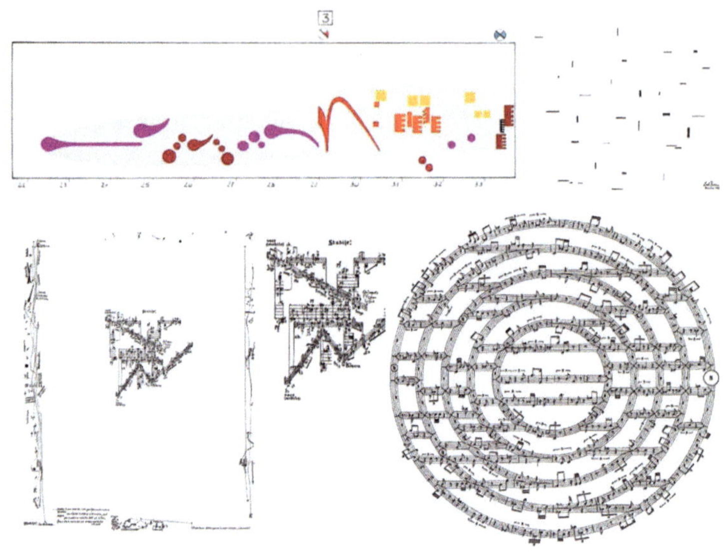

Figure 10: Examples of non-standard music notation systems. Upper left: György Ligeti. *Artikulation*, 1958. Upper right: Earle Brown. *December 1952* (Folio). Lower left/center: Sylvano Bussotti. *Sette Fogli* "Mobile-Stabile per Chitarre, Canto e Piano", 1959. Lower Right: Mestres Quadreny. *L'Estro Aleatorio*, 1973-78.

The ambiguity of the description can not ensure precision in the final result of the production process; however, it is accepted as valid proof of the artwork authenticity. Only the holder of this certificate may produce the wall painting and sell it.

Figure 14 shows two execution diagrams, made at different moments, for the correct processual interpretation of the artwork. It is apparent that they are different reinterpretations and variations of the same *plan*. This type of instruction diagram does not satisfy Goodman's requirements. The generated state of authenticity I is never the same, and furthemore is ephemeral.

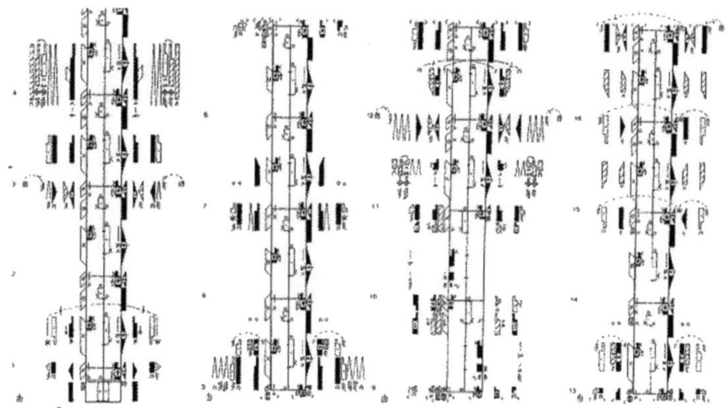

Figure 11: Example of *labanotation*: a dance notation system.

The New Media Art Conservation Theory lays out a notation system as a *proof of authenticity*, in the form of a symbolic system representation of information (`A3`, for example). A *proof of authenticity* that safeguards the *discernible differences* of the Restoration object. A notation system that allows the recreation of the system-object for the symbol-object to remains unchanged. *Identity*, in terms of *discernible differences* does not give rise to subjectivity, and conserving the *symbolic value* of an artwork is not about maintaining the extrinsic values given to it. "Restoration is defined according to its objects" [Muñoz Viñas, 2003]; it is about maitaining its discernible intrinsic values. *Non-discernible* properties act as glorified powers that can lead irrevocably to *fetishism*. The Restorer must extract and understand these values (an interview with the artist can be a very valuable tool for this purpose) but the reinterpretation of the symbolic value can lead to failed states of authenticity, even falsification.

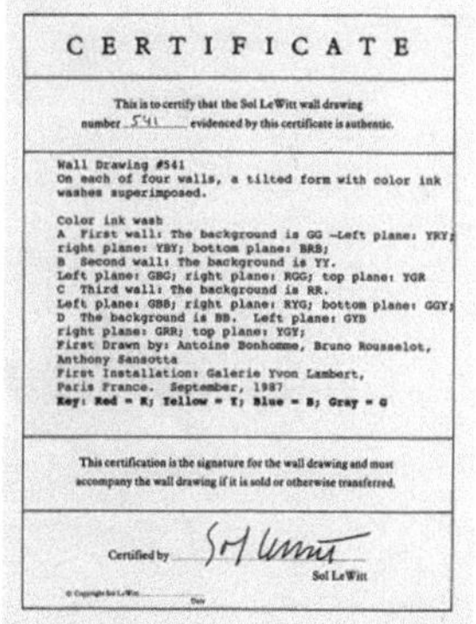

CERTIFICATE

This is to certify that the Sol LeWitt wall drawing number 541 evidenced by this certificate is authentic.

Wall Drawing #541
On each of four walls, a tilted form with color ink washes superimposed.

Color ink wash
A First wall: The background is GG -Left plane: YRY; right plane: YBY; bottom plane: BRB;
B Second wall: The background is YY.
Left plane: GBG; right plane: RGG; top plane: YGR
C Third wall: The background is RR.
Left plane: GBB; right plane: RYG; bottom plane: GGY;
D The background is BB. Left plane: GYB
right plane: GRR; top plane: YGY;
First Drawn by: Antoine Bonhomme, Bruno Rousselot, Anthony Sansotta
First Installation: Galerie Yvon Lambert, Paris France. September, 1987
Key: Red = R; Yellow = Y; Blue = B; Gray = G

This certification is the signature for the wall drawing and must accompany the wall drawing if it is sold or otherwise transferred.

Certified by Sol LeWitt

Sol LeWitt

Date

Figure 12: *Wall Drawing* #541, Sol LeWitt. *Plan* for the production of the drawing, which in turn serves as authentication certificate.

Figure 13: *Wall Drawing* #541, Sol LeWitt. Production for the Virginia Museum of Fine Arts in 2008.

Heisenberg attributed the following quote to Niels Bohr (both men were very prominent and influential quantum physicists), while on a stroll through Krönberg Castle.

> Isn't it strange how this castle changes when we remember that Hamlet lived in it? As scientists, we believe that a castle is a simple stone construction and we admire the architect who designed it. The stones, the green roof with its patina, the carvings in the chapel, are what make up the castle. Suddenly, the walls and the ramparts speak a different language [...] Yet all we know about Hamlet is that his name appears in a 13th century chronicle [...] everyone knows the questions that Shakespeare had him as, the depth of human nature he was made to reveal to us, and so he too had to be given a place under in the sun, here in Krönberg.

This experience can have many interpretations. Firstly, its questions of the meaning of *reality*. Yet it also illustrates the essence of *symbolic value*. *Contemplation* is directed by our experience and experience is active grasping. *Perception* evolves and changes at every moment.

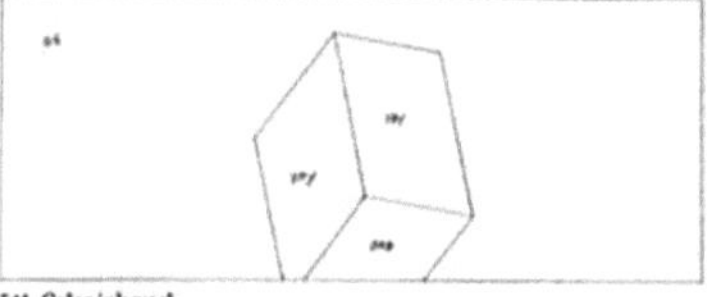

541. Color ink wash
A. First wall: The background is gray, gray. Left plane – yellow, red, yellow; right plane – yellow, blue, yellow; bottom plane - blue, red, blue;

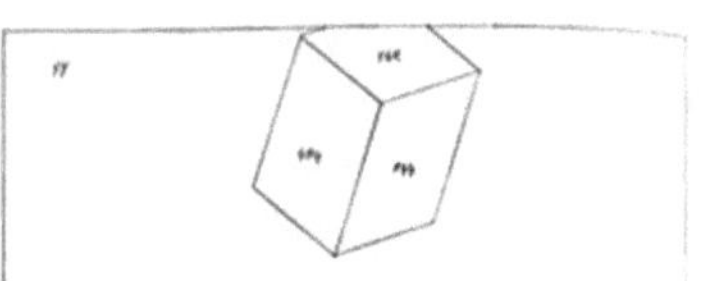

B. Second wall: The background is yellow, yellow. Left plane – gray, blue, gray; right plane – red, gray, gray; top plane – yellow, gray, red;

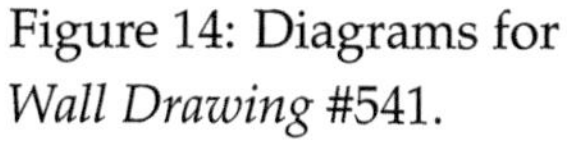

Figure 14: Diagrams for *Wall Drawing* #541.

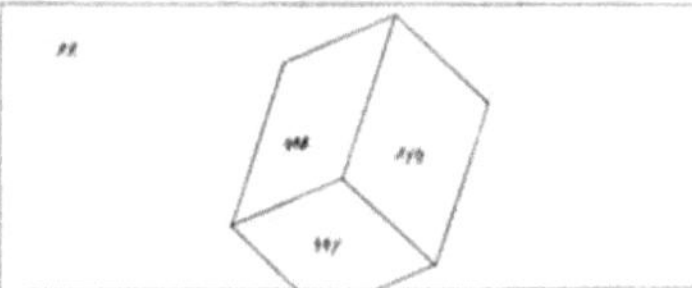

C. Third wall: The background is red, red. Left plane - gray, blue, blue; right plane – red, yellow, gray; bottom plane - gray, gray, yellow;
D. The background is blue, blue. Left plane – gray, yellow, blue; right plane – gray, red, red; top plane – yellow, gray, yellow

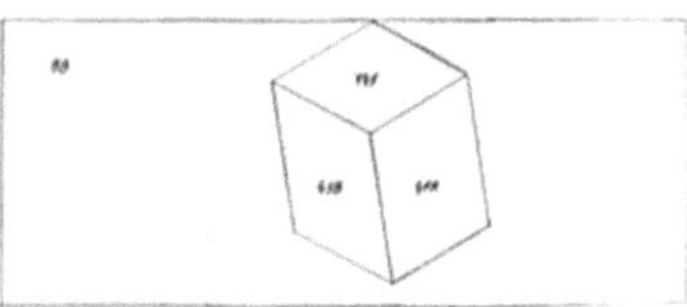

First Drawn by: Antoine Bonhomme, Bruno Rousselot, Anthony Sansotta
First Installation: Galerie Yvon Lambert, Paris, France
September, 1987
First and second walls: 190 x 510" (475 x 1275cm)
Third and fourth walls: 90 x660" (475 x 1650cm)

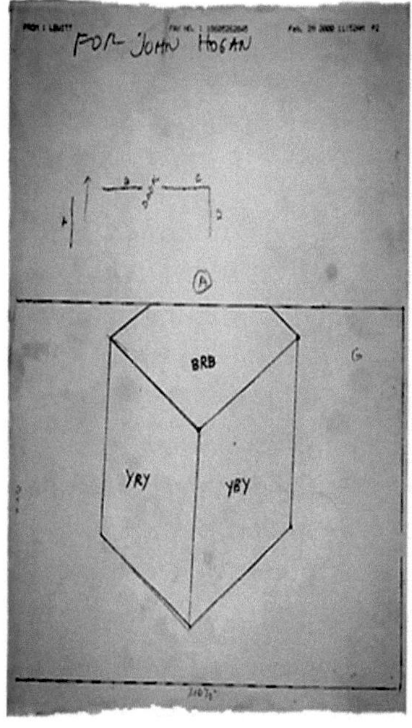

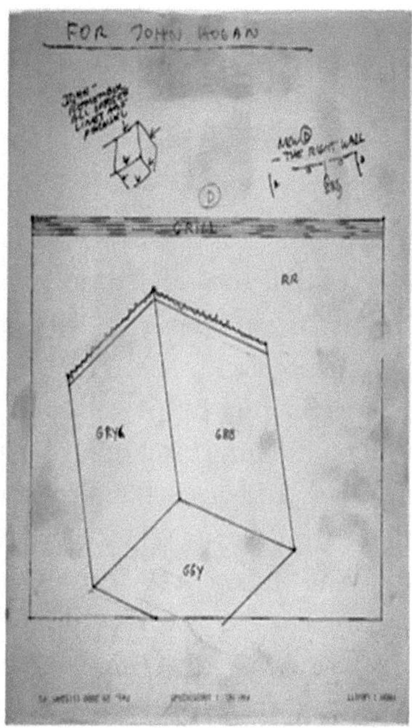

For Illya Prigogine, winner of the Nobel Prize in Chemistry, it is not possible to separate the problem of reality from that of human existence:

> What is Castle of Krönberg, independient to the questions we put to it? The stones speak to us of their molecules, the geological strata they were quarried from, perhaps the extinct species they contain in fossils form, of the cultural influences that worked on the architect, or the questions that pursued Hamlet to his death. None of this matters are arbitrary, nor do they permit us to sidestep preference to Hamlet, whose presence here gives them meaning.

Krönberg Castle has a value in relation to its *discernible differences* and another, probably greater, in relation to its *non-discernible differences*; but the latter is not an aesthetic (intrinsic) value but a symbolic (extrinsic) one. Perhaps *historicity* is not given by these *non-discernible differences* that are extrinsic to the object.

> In a narrower sense, historicity will involve the interpretation of temporality, which is the characteristic of transpired events that occur in the course of time, of past events [DefiniciónABC, 2010].

Historicity is a kind of reflection on the temporality of the events that took place on the object, and it is relative. If historicity is any question, thing or person that has the quality of being historical, i.e. that it is relative or part of history, and history is the interpreted facts and is said to be relative, so too will be the interpretation of history, which is *historicity*.

One could go further and try to extend the analysis of authenticity from *mental representations*, understood as that material or symbolic form to account for something real in its absence, organized into structures that make it possible to make sense of the world.

If C is the mental representation of the source (pattern of comparison and recognition), A is the mental representation of the source as a receiver and B the mental representation of the receiver (not including the source), then C will likely be equal to A. Were this the case, then by carrying out the creative project, an object whose mental representation matches the expectation can be generated, though perhaps with a difference in degree. Yet A will still be different from B, to the extent the receiver introduces *non-discernible differences* from the source (which is not possible when source and receiver are identical).

The *mental representation* of a reality, an object or the like is a consequence of creativity. For Marina, "to create is to put mental operations to a creative project." Its anatomy would have different parts: *theme, search pattern, motives, feelings, restrictions* and *pattern of comparison and recognition*.

> An artist set outs to begin an artwork. The artist develops a *project*. What representation does the artist have of the objective at start of an artwork? Following that they say, authors usually begin with a very vague idea of what they intend to achieve. This is what A.I. experts call ill-defined problems.
>
> [...] The project is an unreality to which I surrender control of my behavior. This unreality is often fragmentary, confusing or minute information, that can however activate and direct action, proposing a *goal*. The first component of the project is the *goal*, the objective anticipated by the subject, as an end to be achieved. Except in very simple cases, where the objective is precisely designed, projects contain only an empty search pattern. When I talk about "empty patterns", readers should imagine what it's like when a word is on the tip of the tongue. You're unable to say the word, but you can recognize it when it appears. So, thanks to *search patterns* we create the information needed to fill them, and we look for the plans, methods and operations that are needed.

[...] The project is an action about to be started. Something glimpsed in the distance is not a project until it has been giving a *running order*, even if this order is deferred. [...] The project will activate, motivate and direct the action, and must have enough appeal to do so. At the origin of all project ideas there is a desire to act. This sentimental scheme allows the subject to invent motives for action. Conversely, the cancelling of desire annulment leads to an inability to create a project.

[...] Through action, we carry out the project. [...] At its core one also finds the conditions and restrictions that the subject endures or imposes on itself. Both must be acknowledged, since not all restrictions are imposed on the creator, and many are of their free choise. The goal can be a challenge, as is often the case in creative activity, precisely because the desire to reach that remote area of development relates it to other types of the adventurous impulse. [...] Much of the creative task is the skillful management of constraints.

A project drives and directs action, but some criteria are needed if we are to discern the right movements and know if we have reached the goal. If I want to discover the Indies, I need to know how to recognize them. Every time an inventor, scientist or artist makes the effort to do a project, they must compare each of its steps with the proposed objective. And yet it is the objective that one is precisely trying to find, but it is not known, so the search is led by what is searched, which at the same time is the unknown. This paradoxical situation is resolved by appealing to some criterion that is not the same objective sought, but that allows it to be recognized. Thanks to that criterion, to that pattern of comparison and recognition, the artist will be able, if the time comes, to give the stop command.

[...] When an artist sets out a project –be it a novel about a red-head, or to paint "the demoiselles of a brothel in Avignon"– the subject that is sketched out is accompanied by the artist's system of preferences, which will act as a pattern of evaluation [Marina, 2000].

The stop command is made when $C = A$,[41] right when the expectations or goals are satisfied by the result. But $A \neq B$, so the choice of the *state of authenticity* is a complex task that must start by evaluating the a priori *risk* of an a posteriori Restoration. The *risk* can be determined by how much A deviates from B along any of these axes (i.e. after a multidimensional analysis); but this is a possible B. The risk is the result of aesthetic, symbolic, economic feasibility study that can help define what A *state of authenticity* should be achieve.

[41] When somehow the concrete object perceived by the *receiver* is close enough to the abstract object designed by the *source* in Moore's diagram.

States of authenticity correspond to $A \neq X$ *changes of identity*, despite their *continued identity*. The question is: where and/or when does this transition take place? At what moment does Theseus's ship stop being authentic, and is no longer Theseus's ship? Where do we place the decision threshold? Analyses usually adopt logic as the primary philosophical tool in a kind of analytical philosophy. The use of Boolean[42] logic propositions and operators, the most precise of all sciences and theoretical disciplines, has nevertheless been alternatively accepted and rejected in philosophy from the time of Bertrand Russell and Gottlob Frege at the beginning of the 20th century until the present day; this may be because, in spite of its accuracy, it is not capable of reproducing thought patterns. *Fuzzy logic*,[43] created by Lotfi Zadeh, and in which Boolean logic is a special case, may be more appropriate in that it models lexical uncertainty or imprecision and is very useful for solving problems that cannot be represented by mathematical models due to incomplete data or the complexity of the model [Zadeh, 1996]. This logic could be useful to evaluating the state of authenticity X of an object at a certain instant, with respect to the proto-state A.

[42] Proposition logic is a Boolean algebra.

[43] Fuzzy logic uses linguistic models in lieu of mathematical models "to program" the ambiguous logic of thought, and control processes without the need to model the system.

Morphology

In Restoration, the art object, whether *produced* or *recreated*, has two basic functional elements: *aspect* and *structure*. Their function is to provide *image* and *support*, respectively.

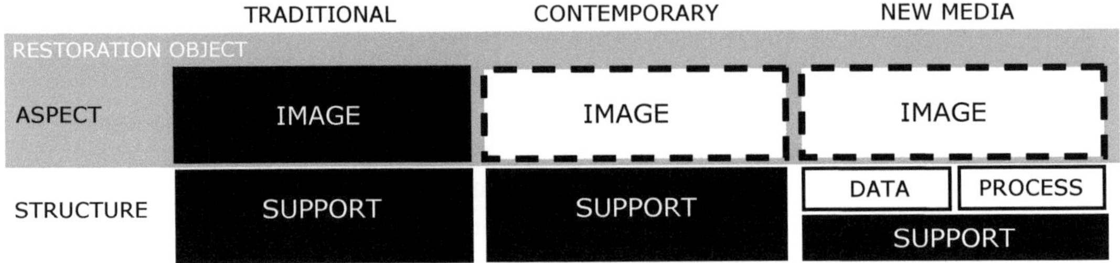

Figure 15: The Restoration object in Restoration theories. In this diagram, *image* functions as *aspect*; it is the aesthetic, poetic, symbolic carrier, etc., while the *support* serves as *structure*, as base, and its value is subordinated to the value of the *image*.

In all *traditional theories of Restoration*, *matter* is the object of Restoration, represented in the Figure 15 by black boxes. *Contemporary theories of Restoration* must consider that the image can be material, immaterial or hybrid, which makes *reversibility* a utopia. *New media theories* of the Restoration also have to deal with hybrid supports. In this case, reversibility is simply a fallacy.

In the Teoria del Restauro, Cesare Brandi [Brandi, 2008], established a functional hierarchy between the *aspect* and the *structure* of the Restoration object that presupposes a subordination of the latter to the former. But the first axiom[44] of Brandi's theory is: "[...] only the matter of the artwork is restored. *Matter* is not to one side *image* to the other." Both concepts, *aspect* and *structure*, require a medium or physical *support*: "[...] they will be two functions of matter in the artwork." The physical media associated with the *support* act as material structure in the transmission of the *image*: *aspect*, "[represent] a media and not an end [...] Matter is presented as that which serves the epiphany of the image."

[44] An axiom is a proposition or statement that is so evident that as not to require demonstration.

The internal *structure* is allowed change, provided "the transformed *structure* does not affect the *aspect*." Contemporary Restoration theories, however, directly question this first proposition, and reveal that not only is it not an axiom, it is also wrong, since "the *signifier* [...] is also a matter of restoration." [Jiménez, 1998, p. 176] Contemporary theories or Restoration must respond to free will. Aside from its aesthetic connotations, experimentation in modern art brought with it a redefinition of the object of Restoration and of the very processes of Restoration. Charles Saatchi's statement that

> There are no rules about investing. Sharks can be good. Artist's dung can be good. Oil on canvas can be good. There's a squad of conservators out there to look after anything an artist decides is art,

says it all. The emergence of materials that are alien to the academic tradition of the fine arts[45] and the disappearance of matter in the image[46] plunged the young discipline of Restoration and the very concept of Patrimony into crisis.

[45] coming from industrial, organic, and unstable processes, etc.

[46] with the introduction of film, be it photographic, filmic, or sound, and the inclusion of conceptual, performative, ephemeral practices, etc.

The excesses of contemporary art are more than "challenges": they question contemporary Restoration. In 1972 the Tate Gallery paid £2,297 –twice the average annual salary at the time– for Carl Andre's *Equivalent VIII*, a series of 120 bricks arranged in a rectangle on the museum floor. In 2000 it bought Piero Manzoni's *(Merda d'artista*, a tin of the artist's excrement for £22,300 pounds (€27,000), a price based on the weight of the tin, tied to the price of gold at the time of purchase.[47]

[47] The tins were put up for sale at a value then equal to thirty grams of gold. Today their price in euros is in the 4-5 digits, on the rare occasion that one of them is sold or auctioned.

In 1991, collector Steve Cohen bought Damien Hirst's *The Physical Impossibility of Death in the Mind of Someone Living*, a shark over four meters long suspended in a transparent formic aldehyde tank, for about 9.5 million euros. Some experts believe the artist was wrong to use formaldehyde instead of an alcohol-based solution.

However, Larry Gagosian, the world's most famous art dealer who also acted as an intermediary in the sale, told *The Art Newspaper* that "the shark is a conceptual work and replacing it with another of equal size and appearance does not alter the piece." Hirst's *The Tranquility of Solitude (for George Dyer)* triptych, inspired by Francis Bacon, uses three flayed sheep. The first sheep appears sitting on a toilet bowl and has one front leg in the sink while the other is pierced by a syringe. The open body of the second sheep (in the middle) is suspended over the sink while a third sheep vomits in the sink on the right.[48]

[48] Bacon painted his most famous and dramatic triptych following the suicide of his lover George Dyer in a hotel room.

With the appearance of new media this functional fracture of the system-symbol-object is more pronounced. Since modernity, anything can be art, and can even itself from its materiality. Contemporaneity acts simply as an amplifier with no limits.[49] Everything –material or conceptual– is susceptible of becoming an artwork, and therefore is suceptible of Restoration. Yet this is not possible. Not everything is restorable, nor is everything equally predisposed to Restoration.

[49] According to Danto: "[artistic activity in the late 1960s] was governed by the principle (articulated by the two most influential artistic thinkers of that era, Andy Warhol and Joseph Beuys) that anything can be an artwork, that the artwork does not have to be in a special way, that anyone can be an artist." [Danto, 2010]

The *Restoration object* is an *artwork* susceptible of becoming a *Bien de Interés Cultural*, or BIC [Cultural Interest]. Any artwork, even any object, can have value; personal value at least, or centuries later, ethno-historical value, but it is not considered a Cultural Interest if it is not of interest (artistic, historical, palaeontological, archaeological, ethnographic, scientific, technical, etc.).

Heritage Law requires the *protection*, *transmission* and *promotion* of Cultural Interes by the *competent administrations* and establishes to that effect three levels of interest: *minimum*, *notable* and *cultural*. In article 60 of Law 16/1985, of 25 June, on Spanish Historical Heritage (Ley del Patrimonio Histórico Español, LPHE), BIC –the maximum level of interest– is reversed for *inmovable* designated for state-owned archives, libraries and museums and the movable goods they keep that are part of Spanish Historical Heritage.

This means, for example, that the building of the MNCARS[50] is a BIC in the monument category and therefore all the artworks in its collections are also BIC, by virtue of the fact that they were acquired by that museum.[51] This is important because as a general rule, the artworks of living artists cannot be declared BIC (art. 9.4) unless the artists agrees to it and the work is acquired by the Administration and, at the same time, any acquisition made by a state museum becomes, by decree, a BIC. My intention here is not to analyze the weaknesses and strengths of the LPHE, but to warn of the consequences of applying legislation articulated to protect "[...] *immovable* and *movable* objects of artistic, historical, paleontological, archaeological, ethnographic, scientific or technical interest" (See article 1.2 of the LPHE), that authorizes the competent administration to make such a declaration when contemporary or new media art is involved. Heritage Laws require acquisitions to be safeguarded, but the problem is in how the thing acquired is defined. An artwork usually has a material support (the system-object), but as we have seen, it is not necessarily the symbol-object as well. In most conceptual and digital artworks, it is the image (symbol-object) that has been acquired.[52] It's worth observing that the list of standards applied is *disjunctive* rather than *conjunctive*. The application of a single standard is sufficient to justify the protection of the work under law. From the moment that a competent administration buys *Meda d'artista*, *The Physical Impossibility of Death in the Mind of Someone Living*, or a *Situations* by Tino Sehgal,[53] it has the obligation, under article 36.1 LPHE to *preserve*, *maintain* and *safeguard* that work. If Saatchi had known art. 36.1 LPHE he probably wouldn't have stated, "There's a squad of conservators out there to look after anything an artist decides is art," and instead said "There's a squad of conservators out there [that are required] to look after anything an artist decides is art" and that a state museum buys.

[50] Museo Nacional Centro de Arte Reina Sofía.

[51] Article 27 also addresses this issue. "Movable cultural interest that are part of Spanish Historical Heritage may be declared of cultural interest. Movable goods contained in a building that has been declared of cultural interest and that such declaration acknowledges as an essential part of its history will be considered to be of cultural interest." Certainly, some degree of acknowledgement is necessary, but no institution acquires an artwork that does not contribute substance to its history, and no competent administration would spend taxpayer's money on a purchase if it were not an investment; the acknowledgement is implicit.

[52] and it requires a material support but it is not the system-symbol-object.It is not the whole, but a part of the whole.

[53] Sehgal is mentioned here an example of a conceptual artist who goes so far as to forbid the documentation or registration of his artworks. For Sehgal "artworks can be repeated, and the core of the work is the experience that the visitor has. This is something that would be lost in a video and especially in a photo. I prefer to offer high quality and precision of an experience, rather than distribute it", he says.

At the end of 2012, on the Museum of Modern Art (MoMA) blog, curator Paola Antonelli announced the purchase of the *code* of 14 video games, the first of a list of 40 such acquisitions to be completed in the future.[54] This act, as extravagant as it may seem, is suited to the dynamics of contemporary art. Francis Bacon understood the conversion of art into play when he said, "All art has now become completely a game." Conservers live in and from this game, and through the authority they are given, are now more prone to liberalization. A liberating game that John Cage explains as follows: "what we are doing is an art of living anarchically". This act once again rearranges the roles of the agents involved in the processes of art. Now it is the *conserver*, alien to the *production process*, who attributes *non-discernible differences* and the *conserver's intention* to an everyday object (an immaterial one, in this example) in order to "elevate" the object to art in an unprecedented process of beatification.

[54] The complete list is as follows: Pac-Man (1980), Tetris (1984), Another World (1991) Myst (1993), SimCity 2000 (1994), Vibribbon (1999), The Sims (2000), Katamari Damacy (2004), EVE Online (2003), Dwarf Fortress (2006), Portal (2007), flOw (2006), Pas sage (2008) and Canabalt (2009). All these programs were not created as artworks but as products of the video game market. However, Antonelli asserts categorically that videogames are art and design "praises the beauty of the design that is not seen, of the computer code, which is what center has acquired" [Martín del Barrio, 2012].

Of course, *game art* is one of the more complex practices of new media art, in that it responds to all of Barreca's three Cs: computing, content and communication. Game art are interactive animations, and are therefore related to *animation art*, *programming art*, *computer art* and *interactive art*; they can be programs (only *software*: *data* and *processes*) or hybrid *hardware-software* with the particularity of being designed to obtain the maximum performance from specific hardware resources: *support*. Practically all the *hardware* of the *software* bought by MoMA is obsolete; however, by possessing the *code*, the Restorer can act on the information not as specific code, but as an *algorithm* or *score* and conserve the *image*; the Restorer can apply, through recreation, the paradigm of permanence of new media art conservation, *permanence through change*.

In new media art the object is disarticulated : material does not constitute *structure* and *aspect*, but only a part of the structure: the *support* and, only occasionally, the *aspect*. The *structure*, besides the *support*, contains two other optional components: *data* and *processes* (metadata) connatural to the new media art and, in general, to a considerable part of the post-auratic artistic practices.

In the digital art *structure*, only the *support* is active material; usually a computer or digital processor in general, which contains *information* in the form of *data* and *processes* (*data* transformers or *metadata*); both intangible, immaterial, virtual [Sterling, 2003].

The numerical concept of "0" and "1" is logical, not physical; but, despite its immateriality, it requires a support. According to Sterling: "if you don't preserve it in some material form, you are not preserving immateriality: you are preserving nothing."*Data* organizes information according to a certain *format*. A *process* is nothing more than a special type of data, *code*, which forms a sequence of execution orders or code to transform data into an active digital support to generate an *image* that functions as an *aspect*. *Processes*, effectively represented by *algorithms*, are implemented in certain programming languages, operating systems, platforms, tools and multi-level virtual machines (with certain technologies) that are highly susceptible to obsolescence.

As a result, it is important to orient the phases of conception, development, and documentation of the works towards their *data* and *processes*, and abstract them from what is perishable, changeable, ephemeral. The decision to conserve the *support*, *process*, *data* and/or *image* is therefore independent and non-exclusive.

The Restoration of the image is therefore related to the fidelity of the aesthetic representation, to the value of the symbol-object. The perception of an artwork on a monitor of a certain technology, brand, manufacturing time, hours of exposure, environmental conditions, etc., is unique. The Restoration of the image, in both cases, can ensure an indiscernible identity in perceptual terms, but these criteria would need to be suitable documented,[55] but it is not necessary as the symbolic value is given by non-discernible differences.

[55] Rare and infrequent; probably due to its eminently technical, sophisticated nature, lack of standardization, etc. It is very important to systematize and *objectify* These perceptual criteria.

One of the areas of greatest "compromise" is in coming to terms with the fact that in much digital art, the image is not conservable.[56]. This is different from what traditional and contemporary restoration theories propose. In "digital art, what is conservable are the data and processes that generate the image: "Digital art is a process-oriented art form" [Paul, 2008].

[56] as when the representation depends on the *process* and/or interaction (e.g., works that include a closed video circuit.

Muñoz Viñas introduces the Mustang paradox [Muñoz Viñas, 2003, p. 38] to question Bonsanti's Copernican rivuluzione [Bonsanti, 1997, p. 109–112] on the characteristic element of the Restoration: *subject* or *object*. Bonsanti's *rivoluzione* accepts that "the characteristic element [of the Restoration] is not in the object, but in the subject." By contrast, Muñoz Viñas says that "[the Contemporary Restoration Theory] accepts that Restoration can be defined in terms of its objects, but argues that what characterizes those objects are features of a subjective kind, established by people and not inherent to the objects themselves".[57] In a sense, the Mustang paradox is a contemporary version of the ship of Theseus paradox:

[57] In other words, non-discernable differences.

> The P-51 Mustang [...] was originally a weapon of war, a single-seat plane manufactured in the United States that played an important role in Second World War. After the war, it remained in service for some time, until it was finally withdrawn. Many of these Mustangs were sold to private individuals, who used them for exhibitions, racing or simply for personal use. Later, as a result of its logical deterioration and mechanical problems, increasingly frequent and more difficult to repair, they were forgotten. In recent years, however, a number of these individuals, and also some museums, have restored some of the old Mustangs to flying conditions. The restoration of a Mustang involves the same type of operations than did repairing a Mustang during the Second World War: replacing the necessary mechanical parts, rectifying cylinders, tightening screws, fixing or replacing weakened suspenders, rewiring as necessary, eliminating dents, repainting, etc. And the Mustang is the same Mustang that was flown in some squads during World War II. Now, however, its repair is no longer a repair, but a restoration.

"What relates all objects is their symbolic character" [Muñoz Viñas, 2003, p. 40]. This reflection is the basis of the Contemporary Theory of Conservation. *Restoration objetcs* are symbols-object. "Restoration can [must] reinforce the symbolic efficacy of an object" [Muñoz Viñas, 2003, p. 45]. The Mustang paradox illustrates that only once an object acquires symbolic value[58] are the processes, task and technical operations of maintenance and repair considered conservation and restoration processes. In this sense 'to restore is to reconstruct", to repair [Moreno-Navarro, 2007].

A *Restoration object* in digital art has a dual character, like the P51: it is an system-object that, because of its inclusion in the art circuit;[59] be it a *Brillo Box*, Krönberg's castle, the embalmed sheep of *Tranquility of Solitude* or the P-51.

Only the pretense of function, should it have one, distinguishes it from the symbol. It possesses an initial symbolic load that conditions it as a symbol-object. As an system-object, the P-51 has to meet certain functional requirements –the "efficiency of the product" in Brandi's words [Brandi, 2008, p. 13].[60] As a symbol-object it must satisfy those functional requirements, but only insofar as they preserve its symbolic value. It is precisely this system/symbol duality in the conception of the object that differentiates it from P-51.[61] In the development and conception of an artwork, however, there is not obligation to conform to a specific axioms or follow protocols, or to guarantee "anything" in terms of utility of efficiency as a system; only as *symbol*.

The system-object is developed for a user, in engineering jargon, or "customer". The protocols to determine the requirements of a system-object are designed to collect information that is reliable, accurate, complete, consistent, and easy to verify and modify.

[58] "Museization [...] can make objects that were not symbolic at all into symbolic objects " but "Restoration does not have that capacity, or has it to a lesser extent."

[59] Whether by museum acquisition or by the values that a group or even a single person have bestowed upon it, the object becomes an symbol-object.

[60] Is it a question of recuperating efficiency or effectiveness? Efficiency is defined in terms of the relationship between resources and objectives, while effectiveness is defined as the level of the achievement of objectives. If the objective is symbolic representation, restoration should be about effectiveness, not efficiency.

[61] The P-51 was designed by a team of specialists, most likely multidisciplinary, in line with the axioms of military aeronautical engineering, with very clear and precise methodologies to detect the functional requirements of the aircraft and design the process for manufacturing, validation, training, maintenance, repair, etc.

The individual developer or team must identify the sources of information, ask the appropriate questions, analyze the information, confirm and validate with the user(s) what was understood from the requirements and finally synthesize the requirements into a document that, once it is approved, serves as a script for all subsequent production work. Nothing should be left to chance or at the mercy of free will.

By contrast, the specifications for the symbol-object, aesthetic-object that it is, are usually ambiguous, incomplete, unstructured, and difficult to verify and modify. They don't have to adhere to any rule, system, or practice. The "user" here is the artist, who is absolutely free to make any decision regarding the artwork. The artist orients and defines the symbol-object; the same cannot be said of the system-object.

The artist is his or her own "master armorer."[62] The development of the symbol-object can be done with absolute freedom by a team, a specialist or even by the artist, beyond the theoretical, conceptual, and formal framework of the development of a system-object. Unlike the P-51, there is no guarantee that a symbol-object will be *well-behaved* as a system-object in the functional terms of stability, performance, cost, technological expectations, etc.

[62] i.e., in reference to the person responsible for maintaining and repairing a battalion's arms and armor. In the absence of standardization, he was a creative craftsman who built (in armory workshops there was always a forge) any broken part of a weapon.

Process –the Restoration object par excellence of new media art– is composed of *code* ("the materialization" or implementation of a certain *process*) and *data* and is characteristically no unique. Multiple codes, with multiple data, can generate the same *image*.

The problem that arises here is, at what level can this conservation be guaranteed without the liability of "falsification"? The algorithmic definition of a process, and even its definition in terms of data flow, is generic; it defines *what* to do but not *how* to do it.

It is the implementation of the process that requires a choice of language, support, etc., and the assignment of a specific format to the data. At this level, languages are not yet written directly in *machine code* (binary code that runs on the computer at the lowest level) but in a set of instructions, symbols and syntactic and semantic rules that define their structure and the meaning of their elements and expressions, often called *source code* (what MoMA bought of the video games). The conversion of *source code* to *machine code* is generally done (except in interpreted languages) through two processes: *compile* and *link*. It is during this process that a dependence of the immaterial on the material, the link to a specific structure, or structures, and the expiration date are produced. The "materialization" of language provokes the link to a certain support (HW/SW) and introduces obsolescence.

This transcoding involves the choice of one or more digital processors, operating systems or control programs, communication networks, development languages and tools, peripherals, etc., and it is precisely these that can fail or disappear from the technological showcase in the future.[63]

[63] A computer, in fact, has an "artificial", "imposed" life cycle of about four years, with a strong tendency to decrease.

What maintains the essence of the digital work, the *source code* (compilable for various architectures or media) or the *machine code*? Note that, in neither case, is there any influence on aspect. However, instead of recompiling the code for the new support, what is often done is to "run" the executable code on a *virtual machine* that simulates the old structure on a new one, when the real problem is the obsolescence of the *structure*. The structure is what sooner or later will fail, age, or lose support. Unlike code, "its parts will stop working, break, get stuck or burn out" [Hofman, 2007]. The *structure*, unless expressly desired of the artist, or as part of the aspect, is invisible; it is a means, not an end, and therefore can assimilate a restorative intervention, or even a migration.

Thinking of the support as a means and not as an end is similar to architectural restoration practices, in which "restoration may require the coexistence of a material that is different from the original but no less authentic in the role it plays" [Noguera, 1996]. Or, in words of Antoni González:

> The falseness of an element (recovered or preserved) should not be judged by the chronology of its material [material cause], but by its fidelity (formal, spatial, mechanical) to the original essence [formal cause]. A load-bearing wall or a vault that works as it was originally intended [efficient cause] is more authentic, even if all its bricks, masonry or voussoirs are new.

This functional character of the *support* is of lesser importance in interventions on new media artworks where the *aspect* of the matter is not altered. The "transformed" *structure* does not affect *aspect*.

The dual *symbolic-functional* character of an object divides the object into symbol-object and system-object. The pillars on which the theories of traditional Restoration are based (i.e. *authenticity*, *objectivity*, *universality* and *reversibility*) don't hold up. The system-object of new media art is ephemeral, unstable, immaterial, complex, and diverse. Obsolescence in the digital age requires an *evolutive conservationConservation!evolutive* strategy that prolongs the efficacy of the cultural good and absorbs technological progress in a natural manner. Werner von Siemens said: "we cannot predict the future, but we can invent it." To this I would add: we can adopt it.

Progressivity, Materiality, Reactivity

The conscious introduction of time in the artwork activates the life cycle of the system-object: beginning-development-end, single or multiple. Matter, the object of traditional Restoration theories, is *passive*, and transforms with the non-reflective passage of time. Sometimes, however, the matter that is the object of contemporary theories, and generally speaking, the matter that is the object of new media Restoration theories, is *active*. It not only allows for, but demands an energy expenditure (be it electrical, wind, physical, chemical, biological, mechanical, hydraulic, pneumatic etc., or any combination of these) to manifest itself and feed the useful cycle of the object. This *progressivity* is provided by the system-object, while also freeing the symbol-object from its materiality. From a structural perspective, the artwork, the Restoration object, is a technological system that allows the aspect of the symbolic systems to become manifest.

The image of cinema, and later television, video, radio, post-cinema (ads, video clips, etc.) and even photography is *immaterial*, *intangible* and *unstable*.[64] *Progressivity* demands the action of the art object. *Reactivity*, *replenishing* and *feedback* implies reaction, either to an instruction (or processual practice) or to the interaction with the environment and/or the spectator and is a type of *progressivity*. The properties of *immateriality*, *reactivity* and *progressivity* are consequences of the intentional introduction of the temporal dimension that is exclusive to modern and contemporary art. New media art is basically time-based art. For Muñoz Viñas, in fact, the increased complexity of modern art is fundamentally due to two factors: *performativity* (*progressivity*) and *intangibility* (*immateriality*) [Muñoz Viñas, 2010].

[64] Some authors [Brea, 2010] make a hybrid, intermediate distinction between the material (image-matter) and the immaterial (e-image) in film; an immaterial image, of light, is projected from a perceptible image on the support; unlike video where the image is produced from unrecognizable information deposited on the substrate.

Contemporary Restoration theories have been extended to address these new challenges and the contradictions and conflicts they introduce vis-à-vis orthodox theories. Contemporary and new media theories, as illustrated on the right of Figure 15, must respond to the "complex" nature of the contemporary and new media object.

The *aspect* can be material, immaterial or hybrid (as in the case of video installations) and the *structure* hybrid.[65] In Figure 15, the Restoration object is represented in a gray box, which also corresponds to the symbol-object. Does this mean that the structure (system-object) is not a Restoration object? No. Without system-object no symbol-object is possible. This framework merely touches on the importance of transmitting the symbolic value to the future. The restoration of the structure is completely subordinated to this order, even in traditional theories.

[65] This representation shows the system-symbol-object of technology-related art, and specifically of new media art. Note that the *data* and *processes* are immaterial (represented in white boxes in Figure 15) and correspond to the information and its processing by the *computational* ingredient of Barreca's model.

Instability, Ubiquity, Simultaneity

Furthermore new media art introduces other elements of the so-called postmodern sensibility: *instability*, *ubiquity*, *simultaneity*, etc., which are less common in contemporary art. Ubiquity and simultaneity imply multiple times of existence-experience.[66] Time-space reality is accelerated and compressed; it determines fragmentary modes of perception of reality. Error, instability, configures order-disorder and hence, new realities.

The term new media is, like many other terms used in art, confusing and flawed. According to Wikipedia:

> In the social sciences, communication and humanities, new media are cultural objects developed mainly through new information and communication technologies. New media not only employ and embrace computational advances, but also networked processes. From certain perspectives, new media are a reconstruction of traditional media to respond to the digital revolution [de Wikipedia, 2014].

[66] *Net.art*, for example, is a ubiquitous, interactive, *(web)site-specificity* (according to Alex Galloway). Hypertext, a type of hypermedium conceptualized by Ted Nelson in 1966, is one of the most important tools for *net-artists* in the creation of their works.

New media are new cultural forms (objects) produced at the convergence with ICT (information and communication technologies). New media are fundamentally information, and specifically are digital information: *code*. To speak of new media art is the same as speaking of "information art", or "digital art", or "software art".

Media are, according to Marshall McLuhan, extensions of man. They shapes and control the scale and manner of association and action between the sender and receivers of the message.

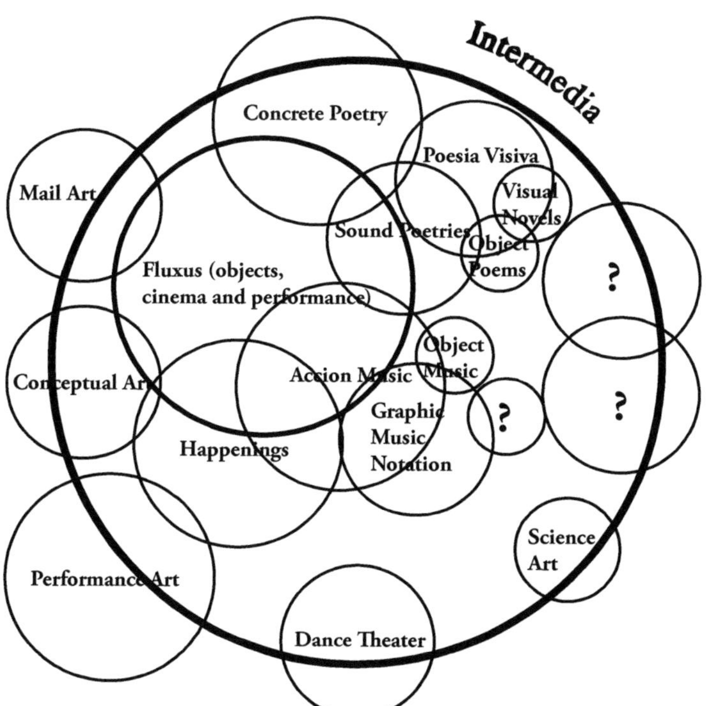

Figure 16: Intermedia. Cartography of media art? In this cartography Dig Higgins maps the practices that break with traditional art and that here I am calling contemporary art. A mapping of traditional art media might show painting, sculpture, engraving, drawing, photography, etc., with little or no interaction among them.

Figure 16 shows a map of contemporary media art. In a sense, this "Intermedia" mapping corresponds to "old media" versus the "new media" in Figure 4; it is a kind of analog version of digital media. "The medium is the message" says McLuhan: the form of a medium is embedded in the message and creates a symbiotic relationship in which the medium influences how the message is perceived. Aristotle understood the medium as the intermediary used to achieve an end, such a transmission of a message that can become substituted (more than *mediated*) by the medium.

It could be said that the medium is, according to the morphological definition of the art object proposed here, that the image carries the message, and the support carries the media. According to Boris Groys:

> [...] the comon usage of the word "medium" is ambiguous: overall , it is used to designate both the media surface [image] and the submedial space that sustains it [support]. The boundaries of this space are vague, and depending on one's ideological conviction, the pictorial image is declared as sustained by the canvas, or "art" institution, bourgeois society, divine inspiration, artistic genius or certain elementary particles or regions of the brain. And yet, when the word "medium" is used in opposition to "sign", it is usually in reference to support, or [...] the submedial space behind the layer of signs that covers the medial surface [Groys, 2008, p. 114].

However, in the presence of empty signifiers: "the media reveals itself [...] as the projection, on the medial surface, of the infinite media-ontological suspicion" [Groys, 2008, p. 183]. The emptiness, the nothingness, generates suspicion; but a belief has existence since "... the thirties, when Clement Greenberg made famous his idea that the modern image not only shows its perceptible surface, but also mainly manifests its hidden medial and material constitution" [Groys, 2016, p. 262] that the medium emits its message and the message we perceive is not only on the medial surface [image], but also in the submedial space [support], even in the absence of empty signifiers. This is true in analog media, but not in digital media. Digital media leaves no trace, it is innocuous and transparent. Any displacement of signs on the medial surface, the image, activates the infinite suspicion of manipulation in the submedial space, the support. But in new media art, the support, metamedium and remediator par excellence, can manipulate by behaving as another media, but not as itself.

The media-ontological suspicion of the medium itself is unfounded. The medium, understood as the submedial space, is not the message.

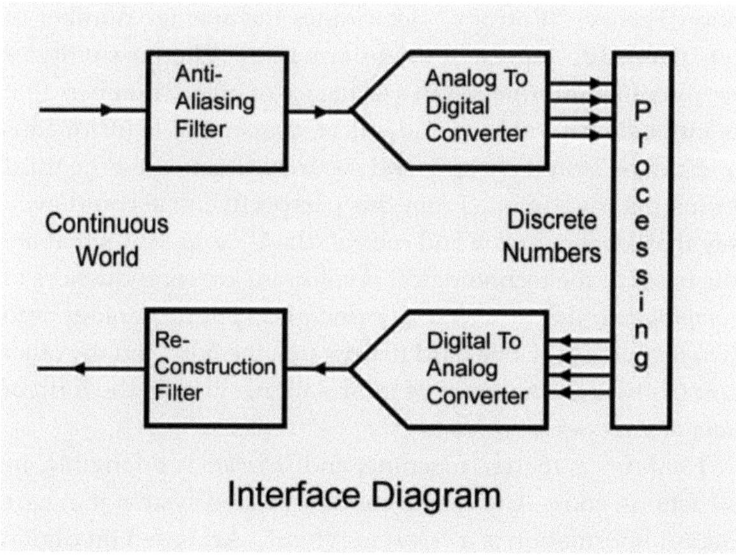

Figure 17: Jim Campbell's Transcoder.

The magic of the new media is in the ability to represent continuous information (i.e. an electrical signal) in discrete information (i.e. a sequence of numbers). In the second half of nineteenth century, Nyquist and Shannon demonstrated that it was possible to "discretize" the information (the exchange element in the systems) without losses to it. This allows the observation, and even control, the real world from a virtual world in a far more economical binary domain consisting only of "ones" and "zeros" equivalent to their analogical homologue.

In *Certain topics in telegraph transmission theory* (1928) Harry Nyquist envisioned the conditions for reconstructing a continuous (real) variable or signal from its (virtual) samples. In other words, the complete information of the analog signal that meets the above criterion is described by the total series of samples resulting from the sampling process. In 1948, Claude E. Shanon demonstrated in *A Mathematical Theory of Communication* how this quantification should be done, in what is know as Information Theory. "Entropy" determines the average number of bits needed to represent the information. The possibility of representing information in a sequence of binary numbers that is infinitely copyable and identical, transmittable (error-free) and can be stored cheaply and securely, accelerated the third industrial revolution. From this perspective, one could even say that *communication* and *content* (the 2nd and 3rd Cs that are the bases of the technological revolution) are consequences of *computation*, the 1st C. These principles split technology into two distinct parts: one hard (hardware), the host, and the other soft (software) composed of information, either in the form of *data* or *processes*.

Hardware is matter, machine, and *software* is intangible, instructions, code. Any media communication system that uses digital information is a "new medium". Art based on digital media communication systems is "new media" art.

Since the late-twentieth century and the early-twenty-first century, contemporary art production at the confluence of art and technology has been mostly digital, with a few rare exceptions; and the use of hybrid devices that allow the interaction of the computer with the real world is therefore considered new media art.

There are many reasons for this, and in the information society, digital is the least costly and most widely available, established, and growing technology (in many countries, including Spain, analog television has been phased out and replaced by digital television).[67] *Digitization* can be seen as an essential domain migration that reorders the processes of Restoration.

A «thing»[68] in this context, is an system-object capable of exchanging, processing and storing code, and is also usually cheap, small and powerful. Before the emergence of "things", a machine was barely capable of processing, storing and exchanging information.

[67] A shift towards total integration into the lives of individuals in what is known as *ubiquitous* computing or *ambient intelligence*. Following Moore's Law, electronic devices will continue to reduce in size, consumption, and price. This is also true for any component of the Cs, such as processors, storage devices and communication systems, which in turn makes it easier to embed and communicate the digital devices in any everyday object and equip them with what has come to be known as *smartness*. Such devices are referred to as "things".

[68] If the thing is a new medium in the age of Internet of Things (IoT), one could speak of an art of "things" in the narrative of Restoration.

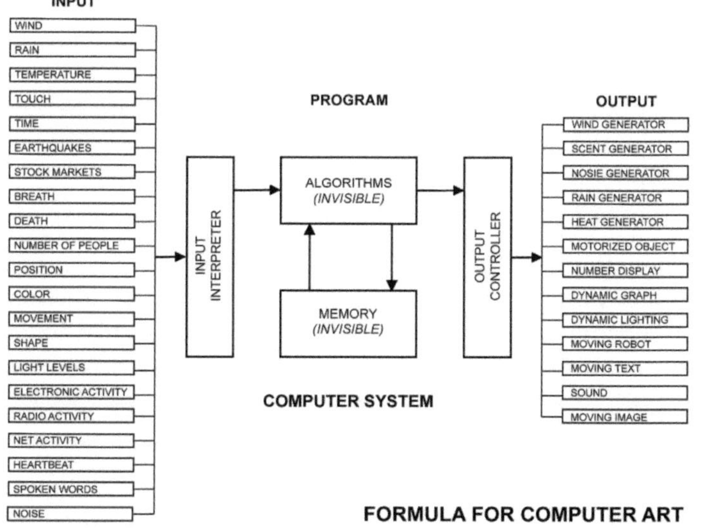

Figure 18: Formula of Jim Campbell's art as a centralized system-object.

Most new media artworks produced with these early technologies were based on a centralized system-object, as shown in Figure 18. This architecture was until just about the 1990s the only "formula" for artistic production.

Figure 19: Formula of the art of "things". The gray circles represent the interfaces with the real world (sensors/actuators). I call this irreducible and autonomous "entity" *cube*.

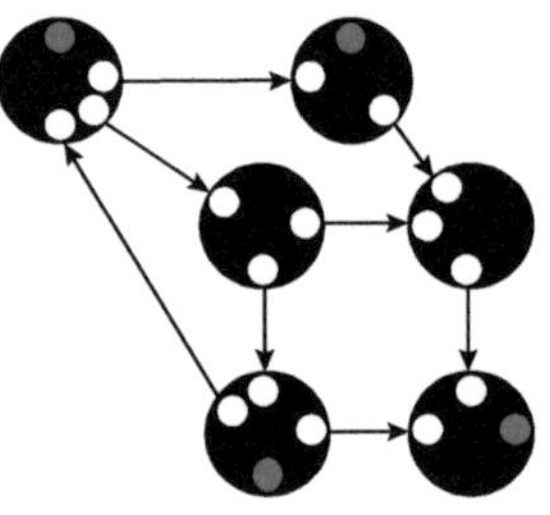

Figure 20: System formed by a network of *cubes*. The white circles represent the *intra* (i.e., inside the context) information exchange interfaces, while the gray circles represent the *extra* (i.e., outside the context: sensors/actuators) information exchange interfaces.

Parallel and distributed computing brought with it decentralization and the possibility of producing much more complex systems: systems made up of multiple subsystems, or networks of systems. Still today, the simplicity of this scheme is suitable for more art productions; however, this type of architecture is fragile, inefficient, and less conservable. The failure of an isolated and monolithic system (system-object) causes the disappearance of the symbol-object.

Note that the input (interpreter) and output (controller) interface corresponds to analog/digital and digital/analog information transcoders, respectively (as depicted in Figure 17) and determines the sensory boundary of the system (context): the continuous/discrete, reality/virtuality, representation/simulation boundary. The functional (intra) level can have a decentralized or modular approach that is not explicit in the figure, between "soft" modules or nodes that function as interpreters (I prefer to call them sensors) and controllers. In other words, it is a matter of creating a small local network between the computer system and the peripherals. The tendency for each input *interpreter* and each output *controller* to carry some intelligence reduces the computational demands of the main computing system and can distribute certain processes to the different nodes, which leads to a primary star-patterned decentralization strategy, where the main node (main computing system), communicates with each of the sensor/controller nodes (and these do not communicates with each other).

Note that Jim Campbell's formula for computer art is an isolated system that does not exchange information and instead only acquires, stores, processes and generates information. With a communication module, one could arrive at a formula that is closer to the nucleus of a complex system-object, a "thing" that is capable of exchanging information with other "things".

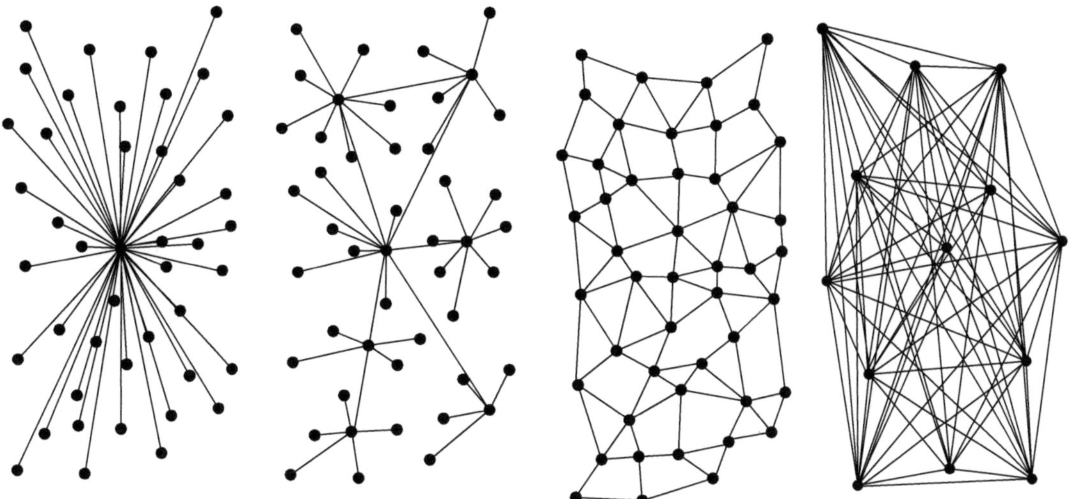

Figure 21: Network topologies. The nodes represent *cubes* and the links between nodes *nexus*. From left to right: centralized, decentralized, free of scale, distributed and meshed.

Figure 19 is an illustration of an open system of a "thing" in the interaction of Barreca's three Cs. This is an «entity», the basic indivisible unit of the support; while Figure 20 is a diagram of a network of *cubes* that interact to behave as if it were one The difference is substantial: this network may be more conservable.

The connection of multiple *cubes* forms a network that can be diagrammed in graphs, as shown in Figure 21; in other words, the communications between the *cubes* determines the network topology. From a systemic perspective, a *centralized network* is an isolated network, a dead system which, although it consumes/produces information from/to the environment, is incapable of adapting itself because it constitutes a single node. Even if the interfaces were intelligent and had the ability to exchange information with the "central" node, its failure would cut off the flow with all the others.

A *decentralized network* is created through the interconnection of the central nodes of several centralized networks, which produces a small ratio of nodes that are highly connected (called *hubs*) and a much larger ratio of nodes that are weakly connected, all with very few connections. This type is also known as a *scale-free network* because its degree distribution follows a *power law* where $p(x) \approx x^{-k}$. The presence of power law is ubiquitous, universal (sociology, economics, physics, biology, chemistry, mathematics, etc.) and it responds to very general, evolutionary mechanisms (with self-organizing mechanisms). Fractal objects are scale-free, they retain the same appearance from any distance, at any scale. The exponent (power) k determines the particular topology of a scale-free network. In non-biological networks (social, economic, ecological, communication and computer, electrical, etc.) $k > 2$, and in biological networks (genetic regulation, neuronal, metabolic, etc.) $k < 2$.

In the *distributed network*, all of the nodes connected to each other without sharing one or more centers. The split between center and periphery disappears and the control of information is weak. A *blogosphere* is an example of this type of network, in that it is a virtual system that "inhabits" the Internet, where *weblog* communities are established. To paraphrase Alexander Bard's definition of a distributed social network,[69] a distributed network is when every node is independent of the rest and lacks the capacity and opportunity to directly alter the behavior of any other node. Seen in this manner, a distributed network is a network of equals.

[69] the Swedish socio-technologist, co-author of "Netocracy" in 2002.

A *mesh network* is a network with maximization of connections where all nodes are interconnected. The high level of redundancy of this type of network makes it unmanageable. In a mesh network, the number of edges (*nexuses*) increases at a faster rate than the number of vertices (*cubes*), which places such a demand on the nodes that it can collapse the information flow.

The functional distribution of a system in a group of *cubes* that share information through their *nexus* depends on the application, but is much more maintainable (conservable), replaceable and upgradable (restorable). The distribution in Figure 20 is *hard*, in that each *cube* is a *HW/SW* system; This distribution can also be *soft*, in that each *cube* can be a function, service, resource, etc., hosted in a given hardware.

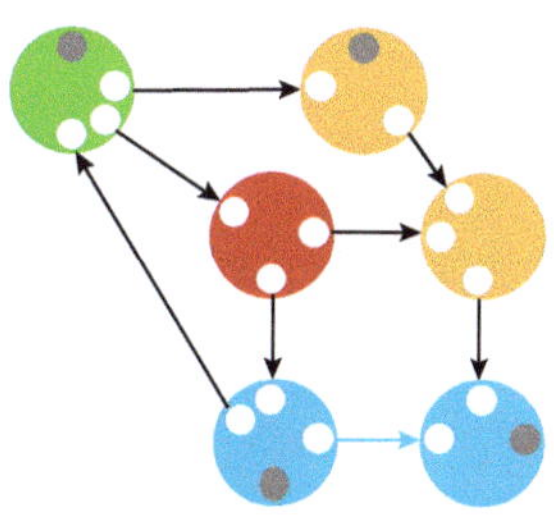

Figure 22: System made up by a network of *cubes*. The *cubes* of the same color share hardware. This is the diagraman of a network of four hard *cubes* (hardware) working as one. Note that only three can communicate.

According to Agustín Fernández Mallo: "Our entire environment is a large set of overlapping networks that sometimes connect with each other and other times coexist without ever seeing each other" [Fernández Mallo, 2009]. This view explains the influence of one network on another and the behavior of complex systems:

> Thus, scales grow from order of magnitude to order of magnitude and, as the famous (if unlikely, but otherwise illustrative) example of the fluttering of a butterfly (node of a biological network) which can have an effect on a cloud (node of a meteorological network) thousands of kilometers away creating a storm, and this storm affects the life system of a community (node of a socio-economic network), and so on.

A complex system-object, a "thing", offers certain "desirable" benefits such as adaptation (related to self-organization and anticipation) and robustness, but there are other attractive features. One property, that is is well-suited to the environment (i.e., art production), is the opportunity to construct a network from incomplete information (states, behavior, constraints). Another, more important property is the capacity for standardization offered the interconnections offer.

Figure 23: A *cube* can be understood as a black box, a thing you know *what* it does through its inputs/outputs, but not *how* it does it.

Figure 24: The LEGO toy is a good metaphor for a complex system-object composed of a network of *cubes*. Small autonomous and modular blocks (*cubes*) are connected to each other through well-defined interfaces (*nexuses*) that allow the construction of complex structures.

The use of a "universal communication language" (*nexus*) between the *cubes* and the independence of the node itself with its connectors to the rest of the network makes it possible to create a system that can mutate, absorb new technologies while preserving its behavior; an adaptive structure with the same dynamic behavior, a system-object that is resistant to technological obsolescence and antifragile. The key, is in the system-object's preparedness for change in its production/recreation within the paradigm of evolutive, permanence-through-change conservation for the permanence of the symbol-object. Note that as long as the *nexuses* between *cubes* do not change, one o more *cubes* can change without anything essential being changed, as if the *cubes* were black boxes.

With the right methodologies, engineering applications such as the development of networks of "things" (system-object) produce predictable, stable, controllable, precise, transparent, efficient, and reliable systems that satisfy certain requirements. The paradigm of complex systems brings with it certain properties that are more useful the richer their behavior, to generate scalable, enduring, flexible, evolutive, adaptable, robust, etc. systems.

`A3` is a methodology that breaks down the Restoration of the system-object into two levels or layers, with one on top of the other [García, 2010]. At the lower level is the *technological infrastructure* (the *hardware*, or *hard* part) and at the upper level the *methodological superstructure* (the *software*, or *soft* part).[70] `A3` does not produce complex systems directly, but it does offer the possibility of them being produced. The production process is guided by a series of decisions made the developer, which are not automatic; these decisions determine the distribution of the final network's connectivity and, ultimately, the resilience, antifragility[71] of the system-object and its capacity to evolve.

[70] The technological infrastructure provides the how of the components and interactions (*know-how*) while the methodological superstructure provides the why (*know-why*).

[71] Antifragility is the opposite of fragility; it is more than resilience or robustness. Resilience withstands shocks and remains the same; antifragility improves.

The production/recreation of a complex system-object is governed by a series of empirical laws known as "Lehman's Laws ".[72] Any Restoration process must respect these laws.[73] These laws constitute the essence of the system-objects and therefore of the art of the new media or the art of "things".

The law of continuous change. In a real environment, a system-object must necessarily change in order to maintain its efficiency or utility in that environment; otherwise, it will become progressively less useful and less satisfactory to the user.

the law of increasing complexity. When a system-object evolves, it becomes more complex, unless the necessary steps are taken to avoid this from happening, or in other words, to preserve and simplify its structure.

the law of evolution (or self-regulation). The evolution of a system-object is a self-regulated process. Parameters such as size, time between versions, number of detected errors etc., remain statistically constant over time.[74]

the law of conservation of organisational stability. In the lifetime of a system-object, its development speed is constant and independent of the resources devoted to its development. This aspect is very important aspect in sizing a project. No matter how great the resources put to produce a work, the speed of execution will not increase.

the law of conservation of familiarity. As a system evolves everything associated with it, such as developers and users, must maintain full knowledge of its content and behavior to achieve a satisfactory evolution.[75]

law of continuing growth. The functionality offered by the systems must grow continuously to maintain user satisfaction and adapt to new requirements and contexts.

[72] In software engineering they are also known as laws of "software evolution", but they are perfectly valid in hardware engineering.

[73] Despite carrying Lehman's name, these laws, are the result of his research with Belady; and the concept of software evolution was introduced by Mark Halpern in 1965, to describe the characteristics of software growth.

[74] There is a limit to the number of changes that can be made within the system before degrading it or introducing more errors, simply because the larger and more complex the system becomes, a small change can affect other parts of the system and cause more harm than good. It is like introducing iatrogenesis.

[75] An exaggerated growth decreases this capacity. Therefore, this average increase must be maintained.

the law of declining quality. The quality of software systems will begin to decline unless these systems adapt to the changes in their operating environment.

These laws are the fruit of experience and are particular to computation, which is the essence of new media. To ignore them is equivalent to considering them as something they are not and to deliberately contribute to the increase in fragility of the system-object.

The system-object or *cube* that satisfies Lehman's Laws is the support of the new media and as such must also satisfy certain principles defined by Lev Manovich in his book *The Language of New Media* [Manovich, 2006, pp. 27–49]:

Numerical Representation. All objects are composed of digital code. A new media object can be described in formal (mathematical) terms and is subject to algorithmic manipulation. New media are programmable.

Modularity. New media objects are grouped into objects at larger scales while maintaining their identities.

Automation. Operations such as creation, manipulation and access can be automated; it is possible to suppress, in part, human intentionality.

Variability. Instead of identical copies, a new media object can exist (or be) in different versions. The fact that the elements of the objects maintain their identities makes it possible to manipulate them in such a way that they adapt, along the way, to the subject (post-industrial logic). Media elements can be housed in databases from where they can deploy their multiplicity (representation, resolution, form, content).

Transcoding. Process by which any medium that is translated, converted, transformed, or migrated into the digital domain becomes, per se, a new medium.

Transcoding is proper to new media communication and according to Alfredo Stipech, it is one of the most important process in its capacity for change and substitution within cultural and conceptual categories, achieving a communication that has the same meaning but a different code, format and categorization.

A conservable new medium has an additional property:

Evolutivity, or permanence through change. Degree of adaptability or mutation of the *parts* (*cubes*) of a system without effect on its behavior as a *whole* (*cube* at the highest point of the scale). A system has this property when it facilitates change of its *parts* without altering its identity as a *whole*. The interaction of a multitude of different subsystems produces the "same" system.

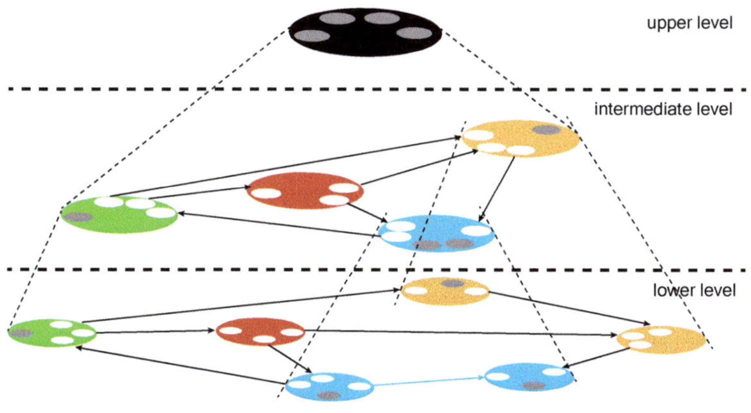

Figure 25: Multilevel representation of an system-object according to the A3 methodology. At the intermediate level it is possible to see how, as long as the *nexuses* between *cubes* is preserved, the *cubes* can change without the behavior at the upper level changing.

Figure 25 is a multilevel diagram of Figure 22. Here, the system is comprised of a network of four hardware *cubes*, visible at the intermediate level and decomposed at the lower level into a larger number of software-type *cubes*.

A system is *part* of the higher-level system and is the *whole* of the lower-level systems. At the highest level one arrives at the system-object that makes up the whole. At the lowest level one arrives at an entity or atomic part of a system.

If in much of the art *production* the structure of the system-object is centralized, much of the *recreation* will entail decentralizing it. The Restoration of the identity ensures the identity of the recreated system-object B on the basis of the identity, at the higher level with respect to the proto-state $A = I$. If this occurs, the symbol-object will remain.

In this scheme the *whole*, at the upper level, is decomposed into its *parts* at as many intermediate levels as are necessary until reaching the lower level, where no further decomposition is possible. At the upper level the *cube*'s interfaces are all with the context, or "real world", and they therefore need to be sensors/actuators. At intermediate and lower levels, the *cubes* exchange information through their *nexuses* with other *cubes*. The conservation of the *nexuses* or peer-to-peer substitution (interface included) will facilitate the change and the adaptation to new technologies while the behavior of the whole system-object will remain the same. In the lower level network, the *cubes* are not divisible; they are entities that must be treated as one and the same thing. Below this level there are only the HW/SW components, the *elements* or members of the *cube*. The entities are the basic bricks, the indivisible atomic systems, the Leibniz *monads*, the uniqueness, on which the *whole* is built.

A system-object thus constituted possesses a special set of properties that allow it to generate robust, efficient, sustainable, antifragile, etc. behaviors and to increase the options for change.

Integrability. Degree of universality of the interfaces of a system. A system (regardless of the level at which it is located) is integrable if it has a well-defined and standard input/output interface.

Flexibility. Degree to which the attributes of the system can be parameterized and adapted. A simple form is more flexible the more it can be varied by setting fewer parameters.

Modularity. Degree to which the members of a system can be separated and recombined. A system is modular when its combination with other systems produces a multitude of forms. It is therefore more advantageous to break up large structures and replace them with many small structures. Note that new media are modular by nature.

Scalability. Positive predisposition to scale up to accommodate an increasing amount of work in an efficient manner. An algorithm, for example, is scalable if it is sufficiently efficient and practical when applied in high-dimensional situations.

The following is a summary of what new media are.

- The substance of the new medium is the "code".
- "New" media will always be new.
- "Old" media are the content of "new" media.
- "Old" media are remediated in the "new" media.
- "New" media will always be superior to "old" media.
- The media (whether "old" or "new") are continually subject to media-ontological suspicion.
- "New" media are evolutive (they need to mutate, to renew themselves in order to last through time) without losing their effectiveness.
- "New" media are "things", objects that are distributed and heterogeneous by nature (the Internet of Things (IoT) paradigm).
- "New" media satisfy Lehman's Laws.

Restoration Strategies

The Restoration strategies for technological art that have received wide accepted and been broadly disseminated were proposed by the *variable media nertwork* project [Depocas et al., 2003] to deal with the obsolescence of a particular medium (through not exactly of a "new medium") of the *variable media* paradigm.

Replacement

This strategy, also known as *storage*,[76] is the most elementary and centers on accumulating as many examples of a given technology, to ensure it remains available for replacement in the event of breakage, or due to wear and tear. This strategy is effective in the short term but is inappropriate as the speed of obsolescence of a given technology increases, and quite bad for capturing the contextual aspects of the works, rendering it useless for *net.art*, among others.

[76] The replacement strategy requires the accumulation or storage of *parts* or the *whole* of a system-object at risk of obsolescence, with all the difficulties. that this would entail.

Some of its variants, such as *refreshing* –the periodic transfer of information from a medium in danger of obsolescence to the best adapted medium–is what Salvador Muñoz Viñas calls *informational conservation* [Muñoz Viñas, 2003]. *Restoration*, which cleans or repairs a file or device when a new version substitutes or replaces the original, is actually related to *migration*; and *network storage*, which uses computers linked[77] by a persistent data loop that keeps critical files in circulation or as multiple cloned copies on several hard disks, is also useful for the conservation of information. Substitution respects the perceptual integrity of the Restoration object, but has a programmed expiration date. Substitution does not represent an advance over the effect of obsolescence, but rather delays it. It is a short-term solution to a long-term problem, based solely on redundancy.

[77] *Cloud computing*, based on services, offers a special opportunity for the distribution of copies or clones of information around the world and ensures the data is protected from natural and social catastrophes.

Migration

Migration is the updating of the format of a work from an old medium to a new one (remediation), to to a newer one (remediation). An example of this transcoding from VHS to DVD.[78] DVD uses MPEG2 encoding.[79] Degeneration or loss of quality relative to the increase in the order of generation of the migration grows exponentially. A third or fourth generation migration is unlikely to meet the minimum quality requirements for "proper" perception of the image.

[78] To ensure higher quality, lossless conservation (albeit not distribution) formats are normally used; uncompressed masters are conserved, while compressed copies in a commercial distribution format are reproduced for exhibition.

[79] Lossy perceptual compression format.

This problem is exacerbated when a comparative evaluation is not possible and presupposes a loss of quality in the interest of maintaining the integrity of the original. In migration, it is understood that preserving the content or information of a work of art, despite the change of medium, is more important, to respect the fidelity of the work's appearance and perception (symbol-object) (which makes this the perfect strategy of informational conservation). In general, the migration of "things" entails the non-preservation of the interfaces (nexuses) of a system-object and does not usually conserve the identity of the symbol-object. Think, for example, of the result of migrating an analog cathode-ray tube television monitor to a digital flat screen television monitor. It is precisely on the media surface, at the interfaces with the "real world", that the identity of the symbol-object cannot be guaranteed.

Emulation

Emulation is a strategy by which a symbol-object is simulated in a different system-object. This strategy is interesting to keep a work alive when its original medium (system-object) has become obsolete, or "phased out". For new media art system-objects, emulation –as opposed to migration– is an option but usually only when the soft part, the code, of the original work is conserved. Emulation uses the same code (software) on a virtual machine in a different hardware. The emulation "program", in this regard, is a kind of virtual machine that emulates the behavior of an old machine and is able to run the same code on a new support [Rothenberg, 1998].

Virtual machinery is a system of systems involving hardware/software that is not necessarily responsible for running code from an obsolete platform. It emulates the behavior of the obsolescent system-object.

Migration entails "mutation", as new formats are developed, while the continuity in emulation is only the responsibility of a *virtual machinery*. Thinking about virtual machinery, in lieu of machine, simply broadens the horizon of emulation, increasing its power.

In both cases, the speed of upgrading, migration, of the virtual support would need to be as slow as possible. This property is one of the most important in the resistance to the passage of time and can ensure long-term support and maintenance. Another equally important property is the implementation[80] of an architecture that has a very high capacity to absorb any technology. Hence the importance of working in environments that are (in terms of the interconnection of systems), standardized, use license-free tools, and propose a standard (or set of standards) for the documentation, conservation, and restoration of technological art.

[80] We use *implementation* rather than *selection*, because there is no architectural standard; it is a requirement, in fact, that meets these needs of the Restoration of new media art.

Reinterpretation

Reinterpretation is the most powerful Restoration strategy, and the riskiest. The symbol-object, each time it is recreated, is *reinterpreted* in a new system-object. In new media art, reinterpretation may require code (software) to be written for a completely different hardware, following a set of specific on-site instructions for the installation, or the reshaping of a work in a contemporary medium with the metaphorical value of an antiquated medium. This is a very risky technique when it is done in the absence of the artist's approval (i.e., when the artist is deceased), but it may be the only way to ensure the re-creation, installation, or re-design of an architecture that is variable with the context. *Duplication* is a variant of reinterpretation that is applicable to media that can perfectly well be cloned. There is no difference between the original and the copy.[81]

[81] i.e., Java *applets* and browsers needed to view *net.art* artworks.

No new media art conservation strategy is without downsides. [Wijers, 2005] presents the main disadvantage of each one. According to this author, in *substitution* (*storage*) "the major disadvantage of storing obsolescent materials is that the work will die once all these materials are exhausted"; emulation carries the possible risk of "prohibitive expenditure"[82] and

[82] The expression "prohibitive expenditure" implies the meaning of "unjustified"; the decision on what amount of investment is appropriate for a Restoration, however, is not particular to new media art.

inconsistency with the artist's "intention"; in migration "the original appearance of the work will probably change in its new medium"; reinterpretation "is a dangerous technique when not guaranteed by the artist, but may be the only way to recreate the artwork." Most ongoing projects work on the development and implementation of description models, metadata standards, terminology definitions for interoperability, compatibility, etc. However, the concept of virtual platform, underlying the emulation technique, can still evolve.

The virtual machine or machinery that recreates the original is, technologically speaking, a HW/SW development able to resist obsolescence.[83] Note that except for *substitution*, none of the Restoration strategies respects the identity of the image that functions as symbol-object, in what therefore amounts to a Restoration approach that "[modifies] the perceptible features of the object" [Muñoz Viñas, 2003].

Muñoz Viñas's Contemporary Theory of Conservation "defends that what characterizes those objects [the theory acknowledges that Restoration is defined in terms of its objects] are subjective features, established by people, and not inherent to the objects themselves." The question is how much respect for the identity of the image plays a part in the transmission of that symbolic or communicative power. What is the margin for a *residue* not to become an *index*, or for the artwork to not become an *icon* in and of itself, but remains a *symbol* of what it represents?[84] How is it possible to value or quantify this difference? To what extent will the image remain the same?

As part of the *Seeing Double: Emulation in Theory and Practice* project, an experimental exhibition was organized to look at the consequences of *emulation* in Restoration.[85] Overall, the experience concluded that *emulation* may be less appropriate than *migration* in the short term[86] and that the artist's intention may be more useful in the Restoration of a work than the search for a universal technical solution.

[83] Obsolescence generates a paradox whose consequences are still difficult to quantify. The technological capacity to manufacture durable products is available, however the need to adapt to permanent change in technology also arises.

[84] Charles S. Peirce distinguishes between symbols (which have a purely conventional relationship to their meaning), icons (which have a purely conventional relationship to their meaning), icons (which in some way resemble what they mean, and share some characteristics with it) and indices (which are causes of what they represent).

[85] The original work vs. version comparison is misleading. Even under identical observation conditions, they are appreciated differently when seen separately than when seen together. Our perceptual system can better discriminate when the reference is total rather than partial and incompletely recorded in memory.

[86] when hardware manipulation is central to the artwork.

That said, *migration*, *emulation* and even *reinterpretation* may be the best options when the adopted technology is prepared to resist obsolescence. The basic strategy must nevertheless be to recreate the work in a robust, well-documented technology that provides all of the entities involved in the conservation-restoration of cultural patrimony (with museums playing a very important role) with the documentation, exhibition, preservation, conservation, and restoration processes; in short, what has been simply called Restoration.

There is no universal solution to all "cases", just as there are no general solutions in traditional restoration or in the restoration of contemporary art (to which some of these strategies may be applicable); however, a methodological approach that preserves the identity of the *image* (symbol-object) (equivalent to identical reproducibility in perceptual terms) is possible through an intervention of the *structure*, in the *support* itself (system-object), which makes the work more capable of evolution, mutation and progress. In this conservation strategy of *permanence through change* I have called this *recreation*, and the corresponding methodology for its implementation, `A3` [García, 2010].

Recreation

Underlying *emulation*[87], suggests a tactic that preserves appearance while resisting obsolescence. This tactic is *recreation*. *Recreation* (a word that comes from the Latin *refectum* and means to remake, reconstitute, or reestablish) and it facilitates an evolutive versioning that isolates structure and appearance and maintains the functional efficiency of the object while preserving its symbolic value in order to achieve a practicable Restoration where it was not possible.

[87] From a functional perspective, *emulation* is a virtual machine that abstracts the behavior of the old support into a new one at the software level; generally speaking, a program that can run other programs that simulate the behavior of the old hardware. In *Emulatronia: Juega con tu pasado*, `http://www.emulatronia.com`, [Consultation: 22-12-2010], for example, it is possible to find emulators of old devices such as the Commodore 16-Plus/4 or Arcade game machines for many "modern" architectures and operating systems. However, recreation is a *virtual machinery* that abstracts the behavior of the complete system: HW/SW.

In new media art, the symbol-system-object is disarticulated into *image* and *support*, and *data* and *processes*, which function as *aspect* and *structure*, respectively (See Figure 15). The *image* that produces the symbolic or aesthetic value must remain unalterable, at least in perceptual terms, while the *structure*, which is purely functional, can and must (is obliged to) evolve. Recreation *emulates* the symbol-object, through the migration (even reinterpretation) of the system-object according to A3, in terms of satisfying the essential requirements and as regards the principal axioms of system engineering. Within Restoration, however, an object- system should ideally meet three essential requirements: resilience to technological obsolescence, a policy of change, evolution (updating) or efficient functional versioning (which can be transferred to good production and recreation practices; in the case of acting on a newly produced or already produced work, respectively) and antifragility (taking advantage of adversity).

In *emulation*, the virtual machine that reproduces the original structure is a HW/SW[88] combination. In *recreation*, the technological infrastructure is a HW/SW virtual machine,[89] that has the capacity to evolve. The methodological superstructure is a sort of notation system with all the advantages that this entails.

[88] with some hardware-dependent portability.

[89] based on the paradigm of complex systems.

Change prediction, management and planning

Obsolescence is caused by *change*, so its impact can only be reduced by anticipating and accommodating change, whenever possible. Obsolescence is the Achilles heel of movable cultural heritage, whether tangible, intangible or hybrid, sensitive to technology (i.e, variable media, new media art, time-based art, intangible art, immateriality art, software art, etc.), which are goods that functionally or aesthetically have technological components.

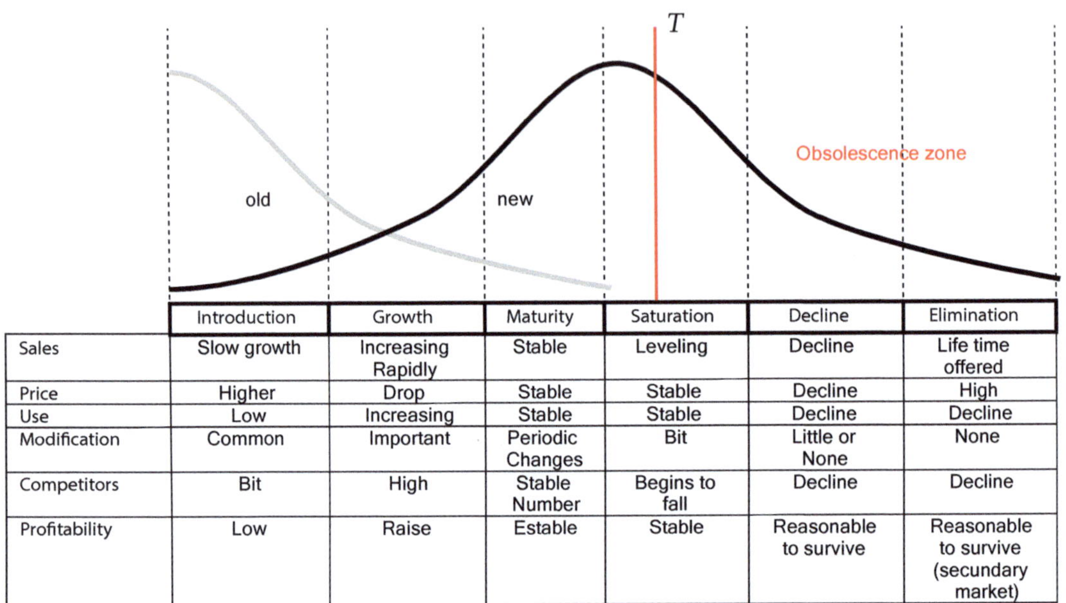

	Introduction	Growth	Maturity	Saturation	Decline	Elimination
Sales	Slow growth	Increasing Rapidly	Stable	Leveling	Decline	Life time offered
Price	Higher	Drop	Stable	Stable	Decline	High
Use	Low	Increasing	Stable	Stable	Decline	Decline
Modification	Common	Important	Periodic Changes	Bit	Little or None	None
Competitors	Bit	High	Stable Number	Begins to fall	Decline	Decline
Profitability	Low	Raise	Estable	Stable	Reasonable to survive	Reasonable to survive (secundary market)

Figure 26: Life cycle of a system of Livingston's six-stage system or phases [Livingston, 2000]. *T* represents the survival time where the event of interest may occur, and during which the system, or part of the system, will become obsolete.

The electronic elements or components of any computing system have a "life cycle". According to Henry Livingston's model, this cycle is composed of six stages: *introduction*, *growth*, *maturity*, *saturation*, *decay* and *elimination*. It also depends on six other aspects: *sales*, *price*, *use*, *modification*, *competitors* and *profitability*; in other words, the shape of the bell is deformed depending on the behavior of these indicators.

An understanding of this model is useful both for the production and the conservation of an artwork. In production, it should help in the design-implementation of the system-object, not so much through the selection of entities, but in the application of strategies that exploit the evolutionary capacity of the related technologies; and in conservation, it could alert to the risk of obsolescence and facilitate its management. The effect of technological obsolescence is not instantaneous; "new" technologies replace "old" ones in the midst of a strong growth-decay tension between the two, which conditions their life cycle.

Problem	Criticality	Solution
Compatible component available	Low	Replacement
Available component not compatible	Media	Migration
Component not available	High	
Requires non-substantial changes		Emulation
Component not available Requires substantial changes	Maximum	Reinterpretation Recreation

Tabla 1: Obsolescence criticality metric.

The "problem" with this model is that it is necessary to know the shape of the life cycle, and this involves an exercise in prediction. It is often modeled theoretically according to some kind of statistical distribution.[90] One can say that the life cycle is determined by reliability, defined as "the probability that a device will perform its function under given operating conditions for a given period of time".[91] Estimating the reliability of a system is very complex. It is not simple to determine how the interrelationship of the parts affects the obsolescence of the whole, though when the system is indivisible, it can be simplified to the reliability of the most critical component of the system. *Prediction* consists precisely in estimating this time, to develop and plan restoration policies with sufficient foresight and anticipation. A more detailed study of how to address obsolescence can be found in *Ergonomía de la obsolescencia* [García and Montero, 2013, pp. 11–21] and *Fragilidad de la obsolescencia* [García et al., 2017, pp. 39–46]. *Survival analysis* may be an appropriate statistical technique because it takes into account the incompleteness of data.

The *obsolescence criticality metric* [Buratti and Del Brusco, 2000] is a very simple qualitative model that relates problems/solutions in dependence of the "degree of obsolescence". Table 1 summarizes the strategy. A non-compatible entity is one that performs a similar function but is not identical to its counterpart. A non-substantial change involves changing some *parts* (*entities*) of the system. A substantial change implies the change of the system.

[90] The Gaussian distribution, for example, is a parametric model that takes into account an expected behavior, not data.

[91] The fundamental objective of reliability is to study the lifetime of a system and of the parts of a system until it "fails", and to predict the probability of failure, the speed of failure and the time at which it will occur. Failure, as the term implies, refers to the impossibility of a system to operate at full efficiency.

DSM, or Design Structure Matrix is a complexity management tool for the analysis of the interrelationship between the components of a system and therefore, to study how the obsolescence of a component will influence a system and, most importantly, how to counteract this. Note that the relationship between the components in Figure 27 can be different in nature: real-virtual, information-mechanical- electronic, software-hardware, etc., making it possible to study the connectivity of the general and specific parts.

Survival time is a quantitative magnitude that wants to be faithful to reality, objective, and free from subjectivity. It acts as a sort of "obsolescence index" on a scale that allows us to assess the magnitude of the disaster before it occurs. It is good practice to make the facts objective, but the survival time or the risk factor of a system only measure one part of the "problem". One could say that they are blind indicators,[92] of the "black box" type (Figure 23, page 77).

[92] They are based only on facts related to behavior over time but do not, for example, evaluate certain intrinsic properties of the object.

How can heterogeneous attributes, functions, etc., be objectified and related? The *rubric* is a very useful instrument to do this. A rubric is a table that has a series of resources (attributes, functions, etc.) on one axis and a weight or scoring on the other.

González, Térmens and Ribera are researchers at the Sabadell Historical Archive and the Department of Library and Information Science of the University of Barcelona who have proposed such a method to evaluate digital formats for video preservation [González et al., 2012]. The question they ask is not when they are going to have the problem. They know that migration from magnetic videotape to digital technology is unavoidable and non-negotiable. The question they pose is, of the available digital video formats, which is the most appropriate?

The formats, the intangible, are the biggest part of the problem; the support and the machine, the tangible, are now a metamedium where technologies and methodologies mix. For example, redundancy and the distribution of resources allows the use of less robust media. Redundancy, according to Amstadter, is one of the main methods to improve the reliability of systems [Amstadter, 1976, p. 317].

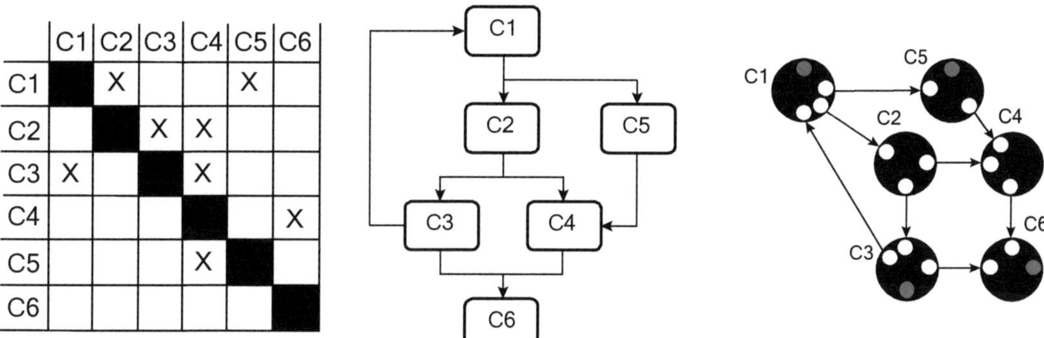

Figure 27: at left, example of a six-component structural table; at center, graph of the interaction of the table; at right, representation of the interaction (*nexuses*) of the nodes (*cubes*) according to the A3 methodology.

The indicators that González, Térmens and Ribera propose to score are applicable to any type of digital medial information and can obtain 1, 2 or 3 points. Table 2 shows an alternative view to the authors' text. The *quality* indicator is meaningless. It is unacceptable that the data resulting from transcoding does not capture all the information in the signal. If it were acceptable, digitizing would be meaningless. Note that the quality indicator has only two possible values. For the indicators to be comparable they must have the same range of values. The reason for the *quality* indicator is that the file resulting from digitization must contain the same information as the original analog signal source; however, the scoring is related to the encoding process to the digital content (some kind of lossy encoding or compression of information) and this is something that is dealt with in a specific indicator.

	3	2	1
Standardization	«De jure» standard (ISO, ITU, etc.)	«De facto» standard with specifications made available to the user by independent organizations or private companies.	Non-standard
Public adoption	Widely used by the user community.	Used on a small scale by the user community.	Rarely used or obsolete.
Industry adoption	Widely used by the audiovisual market.	Rarely used by the audiovisual market.	Rarely used or obsolete.
Adoption by cultural heritage institutions	Commonly used.	Sporadically used.	Never used.
Openness	Accessible and modifiable structure.	Accessible structure but subject to commercial license.	Non-accessible structure.
Dependencies	No dependencies.	Low level of dependence.	High level of dependence.
Stability	New versions rarely appear and when they do, they are backward compatible.	New versions are frequently released but are backward compatible.	New versions are frequently released without backward compatibility.
Interoperability	Wide range of platforms to reproduce the content.	Compatible with proprietary software and some independent platforms.	Only compatible with proprietary software.
Quality		The digital file and the analog signal contain the same information.	Compression systems have been applied to facilitate dat storage and transmission.
Fidelity	Identical result to the original source.	It has been subject to automatic adjustments by software.	It presents serious misalignments and alteratior (color, sound, etc.).
Metadata	Possibility to encapsulate user-defined metadata.	Possibility to encapsulate metadata in a limited way.	Metadata cannot be encapsulated.

Tabla 2: Common indicators.

In my opinion any digital format should not encode or compress the signal with losses. These losses would propagate into any future format. Any format should represent the information as it is. Any future format will be better: it will have better indicators and that is what guarantees the preservation of digital information into the future.

The scoring of each format is a number that results from the operation $i = \sum_k i_k, k = 1, 2, ..., K$.[93] This sum gives all indicators the same weight, but it is very simple to weight the indicators in such a way that $i = \sum_k i_k w_k$ where w_k is a weighting coefficient for each indicator k. For example $0 < w_k < 1$. The best support is the one that has the greatest i.

[93] where K is the number of indicators that are scored and i_k is the value of each indicator.

In this work, specific indicators are also proposed to "detail, break down and define more precisely the quality of a digital multimedia file for long-term preservation using image and sound characteristic values" [González et al., 2012, pp. 292–294]. Such indicators, with the corresponding examination question, are:

Scalability Is it possible to define profiles and levels when saving a file?

Scan mode Does it support interlaced video? Does it support progressive video?

Bit rate What type of bit rate does it use, and can an average bit rate be set?

Compression Does it use any compression algorithm? Does the codec it uses apply lossy compression, and is the loss perceptible to the human eye?

Chromatic subsampling What color space does it use? What type of chromatic subsampling does it use?

Relative weight What is the balance between relative weight and formal characteristics compared to other formats?

Availability of multimedia players Is the playback software easily accessible, is it free, is it commercially licensed, is it current or obsolete?

The proposed indicators may be more or less debatable, but the mechanism itself has great value. Table 3 shows a comparison of some multimedia containers using the indicators in Table 2 (except for quality).

	AAF	ASF	AVI	FLV	MKV	MXF	MPEG	OGM	MOV	RMVB
Standardization	3	1	2	2	2	3	3	1	2	2
Public adoption	1	1	3	3	1	1	3	1	3	3
Industry adoption	3	3	2	3	1	3	3	1	3	3
Adoption by cultural heritage institutions	1	1	3	1	1	3	3	1	2	1
Openness (*Openness*)	1	1	1	1	3	2	1	3	1	1
Dependencies	1	1	1	1	3	3	2	3	1	1
Stability	3	2	3	2	2	1	2	2	2	2
Interoperability	3	1	2	2	2	2	3	1	2	2
Fidelity	3	1	3	2	3	3	2	3	2	2
Metadata	3	2	1	1	3	3	1	3	2	3

Tabla 3: Comparison of the most popular multimedia containers at the time of publication. Although the table does not include it, raw format (RAW) is probably the best; it contains all the data and is free of dependencies. The only drawback is size, but even this is becoming less and less relevant.

Change *management* must study the possible expected changes, how they influence the system-object as a whole as well as the symbol-object, and select the best strategy, with "best" understood as that which restores the identity with the highest benefit/loss ratio. The *planning* of the change is related to the allocation of time and resources for the Restoration.

Change prediction, management and planning of change are mutual man-machine adaptation processes. Works must be permanent as symbol-objects but, as system-objects, they must be evolutive.

The `A3` methodology [García, 2010] proposes the *recreation* strategy for evolutive, permanence-through-change conservation. `A3` is a restoration tool that minimizes or cancels the impact of obsolescence to the extent that it foresees the future mutation and adaptation of the cultural interest. It is built on a technological infrastructure and a methodological superstructure conditioned to mutate, and it can work even from the *production* process. An artwork that is produced by following this methodology is one that is prepared for change, and that therefore can be better preserved, without limiting the creation process [García, 2012].

This scheme of change prediction, management and planning is very similar to the idea of "continuous improvement" and to the idea of quality control designed by Edwards Deming as a four-phase circular process: *plan* (what to do? how to do it?), *do* (do what was planned), *check* (did things happen as planned?) and *act* (how to improve next time?).

The "Deming Cycle", "Continuous Improvement Cycle" or "PDCA Cycle" (plan, do, check and act), form a valid scheme of action to be applied in all management systems (this is currently quite relevant in museums under ISO 9001:2008 quality management and cultural heritage conservation regulations) where implementation and development are related to continuous improvement. ISO 9001:2008 is the basis of the Quality Management System (QMS). It is an international standard for all the elements of quality management that a company must have for an effective system that allows it to manage and improve the quality of its products or services.

A series of tools have been developed to facilitate their implementation of each of these cycles. The planning tools, for example, facilitate and standardize the methodology for planning projects, activities and tasks and help to design products, processes, and services according to the requirements and functions foreseen in the future. Some examples of these tools are: FMEA (Failure Mode and Effects Analysis), Gantt Chart, Pokayoke Intuitive Error Proofing Design Method, QFD (Quality Function Deployment), etc. Some examples of verification tools are: Pareto Diagram, Correlation Diagram, Ishikawa Diagram, etc.).

The implementation of a QMS[94] makes it possible to identify certain key aspects for continuous improvement: *diagnosis* (where are we? knowing the current situation), *planning* (where do we want to go? ability to imagine), *prevention*, management commitment to continuous improvement, the collaboration and participation of all personnel (consensual decision making) and the promotion of interdepartmental relations by establishing a process orientation (encouraging personal development and continuous training). There are many similarities between the quality management system model proposed in UNE-EN ISO 9001:2008 and this evolutive, permanence-through-change conservation strategy. As already stated:

> The Restoration object, in this case, is composed of processes and data, and has a very special feature: it may not be unique. Multiple processes, with multiple data, can generate the same image. The algorithmic definition of a process, and even the definition in terms of its data streams, is generic and perennial; it defines what to do but not how, nor where.

[94] Even the very concept of "quality" has changed in meaning and evolved in an equally changing world. The "culture of quality" is a constant demand in all areas of contemporary society and, of course, in restoration as well [Montero and García, 2014].

This similarity is not accidental, because this proposed conservation scheme is based on the prediction, management and planning of change, on thinking and determining what the work does and not how it does it and is focused on process. Specifically, the methodological similarities are that both are prepared to change and evolve; both propose decision-making based on objective data and are focused on process; making this proposed conservation scheme a methodology based on quality articulated with an action methodology that is compatible with the PDCA cycle and is measurable, evaluable, standardizable and plannable.

There are three types of continuous improvements on a Restoration object:

Corrective Error debugging. This is a must-do process once production is finished. Sometimes it is not performed adequately, due to time pressures, economic constraints, negligence, etc., and when this happens it results in an unstable object. A symbol-object whose efficacy is in fact not guaranteed.

Adaptive This usually involves changes, the generation of versions either to fix problems that were not detected during the debugging process or to migrate (language versions, plugins, changes imposed by the tool and not by the object-system).

Perfective This type of improvement is associated with the evolution of the cultural interest with new HW/SW technologies (and fundamentally with recreation). It consists of modular adaptation processes and, in extreme cases, of its communication interfaces.

There are certain maintainability criteria that must be considered.

Comprehensibility Clarity in modular decomposition. Normally the parts of the *whole* in a system-object are modules that can be interconnected (like LEGO pieces). This favors maintainability. In fact, if you have an object that is not very modular, you will have problems to maintain it. One possible strategy is to modularize it.

Interdependence between modules Minimization of the effects on the environment. The *whole* also relates to a larger whole where it coexists: the *environment*. The more independent the modules are from each other, the more robust they will be against environment changes. "Environment" here means not only the "real world" that consumes, processes, and produces the object, but also the technological reality itself. For example, changes in communication standards, changes in software technologies, changes in paradigms, etc.

Style Use of languages with visibility control and module packaging. Packaging or encapsulation makes it possible to hide/show certain modules or sets of modules. This can be important for security, for example. Encapsulation produces a certain level of abstraction: it considers a *whole*, or a set of wholes at a lower level.

Testing facility Testing during the production process. It is very important that the technology can test itself to debug errors.

Expandability Thinking about extensions from the definition. It is necessary to detect the parts most vulnerable to change (not only technological, but also in the evolution of the artwork).

Documentation Legibility of documentation. Provision of perfective strategies. A well-documented system is a system that can evolve. Documentation should be concise, unambiguous, and detailed. System-objects are normally designed to satisfy certain requirements; this is the starting point. There must be a clear and precise relationship between modules and requirements.

In summary, in the Conservation Theory proposed here:

- Information is imperishable; it does not get worn down.
- Restoration must begin from the moment of *production.*
- In *recreation,* fragility is corrected, to restore the effectiveness of a product of human activity but with an antifragile structure, prepared to absorb any future change, immune to obsolescence. This is a qualitatively superior strategy to substitution, emulation and reinterpretation.
- Instability acts to the detriment of permanence.
- Methodology is an option. The most important thing is not where you get things from, but where you take them.
- Restoration is itself a topologically determined process of reproduction; reproduction guarantees identity by the context in which it is reproduced.
- The norm, the standard, is the philosopher's stone of modularity. Modularity determines the degree to which the *parts* of a system can be separated and recombined. It is only possible to interconnect what you know exactly what it is, what it does and how it interacts.
- Evolutive conservation is a methodology that exploits the value of the standard. It may not be a standard, but one of its aims is to become one.

- An antifragile production facilitates an antifragile restoration.
- A fragile production must be recreated in an antifragile object. An object that benefits from change.
- *Evolutivity* is the term and concept used here to mean the degree of adaptability or mutation of the *parts* of a system without affecting its behavior as a *whole*.
- Any Restoration process has to respect Lehman's Laws. These laws constitute the essence of new media system-objects and therefore of new media art or the art of "things".
- A system is evolutive when it facilitates change in its *parts* without altering its identity as a *whole*. The interaction of a multitude of different subsystems produces the "same" system.
- The IoT paradigm is evolutive. "Things" are, by definition, modular, integrable, flexible, scalable and antifragile.
- Even when a new media artwork is autographic (only one original is produced) its essence is eminently allographic.
- A notation system is a language, a system of symbols that represent a set of symbols, they are codes that require standardization or normalization to be shared. And as a language it is defined by a syntax or grammar.
- `A3` is a notation system for new media artworks.
- `A3` is an evolutive conservation methodology.
- `A3` is modular, scalable, and universal, and based on an open interconnection and integration model. It elaborates the levels of abstraction in the upper hierarchy of Bloom's taxonomy: analysis, synthesis and evaluation.

- `A3` offers artists, specialists, curators, conservers, etc. a tool for analysis and synthesis (evaluation and production).
- The *technological infrastructure* of the `A3` methodology is resistant to obsolescence, and deals with change.
- The *methodological superstructure* of the `A3` methodology is a production tool, useful for the restoration of the work; it is based on the paradigm of complex systems and ensures the evolutive conservation of the object.
- In an `A3` system the nodes are called *cubes* and the links are called *nexus*.
- The magic of `A3` is to maintain the interfaces between the *nexuses*.
- The logical model of the object of restoration, of the methodological superstructure, corresponds to the *proto-state*. It defines the *what* of the system (*what it does, what it is*), without taking into account *how*. It operates on a certain technological infrastructure, it needs it, but it does not suffer from obsolescence like this one.
- The proto-state should serve as a communication tool between all the agents involved: artist, conservator, restorer, etc., and as a guide in all restoration actions.
- The proto-state must define an evolutive conservable solution. Not all solutions are conservable and not all solutions are equally conservable.
- The proto-state presents a description of the *parts*, the relationship between the *parts* and the relationship with the *context*. This is a basic requirement of modularity.

- The `A3` is suitable for solving incomplete problems, learning to learn (which fosters transdisciplinary activity), identifying learning needs, facilitating and encouraging teamwork, assigning roles within the team, specifying work rules, etc.
- Change is good; the result of change may be antifragile but without change the fragile will remain fragile.

Bibliography

Variable media network. URL `http://www.variablemedia.net`.

A.A.V.V. Carta de brasilia, 1995. URL `http://www.icomoscr.org/doc/teoria/VARIOS.1995.carta.brasilia.sobre.autenticidad.pdf`.

Bertram L. Amstadter. *Matemáticas de la fiabilidad*. Editorial Reverté, 1976.

Laura Barreca. *The International Debate around Conservation and Documentation of New Media Art 1995-2007*. PhD thesis, University of Tuscia, Viterbom, Italy, 2008.

Giorgio Bonsanti. Riparare i'arte. *OPD Restauro*, (9), 1997.

Cesare Brandi. *Teoría de la Restauración*. Alianza Editorial, 2008.

José Luis Brea. *Las 3 eras de la imagem: imagen-materia, film, e-image*. AKAL, 2010.

Marco Buratti and Daniele Del Brusco. The obsolescence management based on a "pro-active" approach in conjunction with a "pre-planned" technology insertion route. In *RTO SCI Symposium on "Strategies to Mitigate Obsolescence in Defense SystemsUsing Commercial Components"*, Budapest, Octubre 2000.

Paulina Chamorro. Territorio ausente, Abril 2011. URL http://territorioausente.blogspot.com.es/p/investigacion.html.

Arthur C. Danto. *Después del fin del arte. El arte cotemporáneo y el linde de la historia*. Estética. Paidós, 2010.

Colaboradores de Wikipedia. Nuevos Medios, Noviembre 2014. URL http://es.wikipedia.org/w/index.php?title=Nuevos_medios&oldid=75298602.

DefiniciónABC. Definición de historicidad, Enero 2010. URL http://www.definicionabc.com/historia/historicidad.php.

Gilles Deleuze. *La imagen–movimiento. Estudios sobre cine 1*. Barcelona: Paidós Comunicación, 1983.

Gilles Deleuze. *La imagen–tiempo. Estudios sobre cine 2*. Barcelona: Paidós Comunicación, 1985.

Alain Depocas, Jon Ippolito, and Caitlin Jones, editors. *Permanence through change: The Variable Media Approach*. Guggenheim Museum Publications and The Daniel Langlois Foundation for Art, Science, and Technology, 2003.

Agustín Fernández Mallo. *Postpoesía: hacia un nuevo paradigma*. Anagrama, 2009.

Haroldo Gallo. Patrimonio, autenticidad e identidad. In *Actas del X Congreso Internacional CICOP 2010 - Rehabilitación del Patrimonio Arquitectónico y Edificación. Perspectivas contemporánes y nuevas dimensiones del patrimonio*. CICOP Chile, 2010.

Lino García. *Conservación y restauración de arte digital*. PhD thesis, Universidad Europea de Madrid, 2010. URL https://www.researchgate.net/publication/275769039_Conservacion_y_Restauracion_de_Arte_Digital.

Lino García. La producción como proceso de Restauración. Casos de estudio. Hans Haacke: *News* y *Poll*. In *Conservación de Arte Contemporáneo 13ª Jornada*, pages 301–315. Museo Nacional Centro de Arte Reina Sofía. Departamento de Conservación–Restauración, Febrero 2012.

Lino García and Pilar Montero. Ergonomía de la obsolescencia. In *14ª Jornadas de Conservación de Arte Contemporáneo*, pages 11–21, Madrid, Febrero 2013. Museo Nacional Centro de Arte Reina Sofía.

Lino García, Pilar Montero, and Diego Mellado. Fragilidad de la obsolescencia. In *18ª Jornadas de Conservación de Arte Contemporáneo*, pages 39–46, Madrid, Febrero 2017. Museo Nacional Centro de Arte Reina Sofía.

David González, Miquel Teémens, and Mireia Ribera. Modelo de indicadores para evaluar los formatos digitales para la preservación de vídeo. *Revista Española de Documentación Científica*, 35(2):281–297, Abril 2012.

Nelson Goodman. *Los lenguajes del arte. Una aproximación a la teoría de los símbolos*. Estética. Paidós, 2010.

Boris Groys. *Bajo sospecha. Una fenomenología de los medios*. PRE-TEXTOS, 2008.

Boris Groys. *Introducción a la antifilosofía*. Eterna Cadencia, Buenos Aires, Argentina, 2016.

Vanina Hofman. Album inestable. un acercamiento a la conservación del arte electrónico. *Arte Electrónico/Entornos cotidianos, colección Papers per a Debat N 5, FUNDIT – Escuela Superior de Diseño ESDi, Sabadell*, 2007.

Alfonso Jiménez. Enmiendas parciales a la teoría del restaurao (ii). *Loggia: Arquitectura y Restauración*, (5):12–29, 1998.

Henry Livingston. Geb1: Diminishing manufacturing sources and material shortages (dmsms) management practices. In *Proceedings of the DMSMS Conference*, pages 21–24, 2000.

Lev Manovich. *El lenguaje de los nuevos medios de comunicación*. Ediciones Paidós Ibérica, Abril 2006.

Joseph Margolis. Adiós a danto y a goodman. *A Parte Rei. Revista de Filosofía*, 29, 2003.

José Antonio Marina. *Elogio y refutación del ingenio*. Anagrama, 1992.

José Antonio Marina. *Teoría de la Inteligencia Creadora*. Anagrama, 2000.

Javier Martín del Barrio. El moma compra 'tetris', Noviembre 2012. URL `http://tecnologia.elpais.com/tecnologia/2012/11/30/actualidad/1354276516_786955.html`.

Pilar Montero and Lino García. Gestión de calidad y conservación de patrimonio. In *15ª Jornadas de Conservación de Arte Contemporáneo*, pages 167–178, Madrid, Febrero 2014. Museo Nacional Centro de Arte Reina Sofía.

F Richard Moorer. *Elements of Computer Music*. Prentice–Hall, 1990.

Antoni González Moreno-Navarro. Restaurar es reconstruir. a propósito del nuevo monasterio de sant llorentç de guardiola de berguedà (barcelona). *e-rph*, (1), 2007.

Salvador Muñoz Viñas. *Teoría contemporánea de la Restauración*. Patrimonio Cultural. Síntesis, Madrid, España, 2003.

Salvador Muñoz Viñas. The artwork that became a symbol of itself: reflections on the conservation of modern art. In *Theory and Practice in the Conservation of Modern and Contemporary Art*, Hornemann Institute, pages 11–22. Archetype Publications Ltd; Bilingual edition, 2010.

Jean Newlove and John Dalby. *LABAN for all*. Nick Hern Books, 2008.

Juan F Noguera. Restaurar ¿es todavía posible? *Loggia: Arquitectura y Restauración*, (1):6–15, 1996.

Walter Oppenheimer. Damien hirst o el arte de ganar (mucho) dinero. *El País*, Abril 2012.

Christiane Paul. *New Media in the White Cube and Beyond. Curatorial Models for Digital New Media in the White Cube and Beyond. Curatorial Models for Digital Art*. University of California Press, 2008.

Jeff Rothenberg. Avoiding technological quicksand: Finding a viable technical foundation for digital preservation, 1998. URL `http://www.clir.org/pubs/reports/rothenberg/contents.html`.

Bruce Sterling. Digital decay. In Alain Depocas, John Ippolito, and Caitlin Jones, editors, *Permanence through change: The Variable Media Approach*, 2003.

Daniel Tubau. *Nada es lo que es. El problema de la identidad*. Devenir, 2012.

Gaby Wijers. Preservation and/or documentation; the conservation of media art, 2005. URL `http://www.montevideo.nl/en/nieuws/detail.php?archief=&id=72`.

Lotfi A Zadeh. *Fuzzy Sets, Fuzzy Logic, Fuzzy Systems*. World Scientific Press, 1996.

Index